Math in FOCUS®
Singapore Math®
by Marshall Cavendish

Workbook

Consultant and Author
Dr. Fong Ho Kheong

Authors
Chelvi Ramakrishnan and Gan Kee Soon

U.S. Consultants
Dr. Richard Bisk, Andy Clark, and Patsy F. Kanter

mc Marshall Cavendish
Education

U.S. Distributor

Houghton
Mifflin
Harcourt

COMMON CORE

© Copyright 2009, 2013 Edition Marshall Cavendish International (Singapore) Private Limited
© 2014 Marshall Cavendish Education Pte Ltd

Published by Marshall Cavendish Education
Times Centre, 1 New Industrial Road, Singapore 536196
Customer Service Hotline: (65) 6213 9444
US Office Tel: (1-914) 332 8888 | Fax: (1-914) 332 8882
E-mail: tmesales@mceducation.com
Website: www.mceducation.com

Distributed by
Houghton Mifflin Harcourt
222 Berkeley Street
Boston, MA 02116
Tel: 617-351-5000
Website: www.hmheducation.com/mathinfocus

First published 2009
2013 Edition

Math in Focus® Grade 4 Workbook A
ISBN 978-0-669-01328-3

Printed in Singapore

16 17   1401   18
4500716893   A B C D E

Contents

1 Place Value of Whole Numbers

Practice 1	Numbers to 100,000	1
Practice 2	Numbers to 100,000	3
Practice 3	Comparing Numbers to 100,000	7

Math Journal: Reading and Writing Math 11
Put on Your Thinking Cap! Challenging Practice 13
Put on Your Thinking Cap! Problem Solving 14

2 Estimation and Number Theory

Practice 1	Estimation	15
Practice 2	Factors	21
Practice 3	Multiples	27

Put on Your Thinking Cap! Challenging Practice 31
Put on Your Thinking Cap! Problem Solving 33

Cumulative Review for Chapters 1 and 2 35

3 Whole Number Multiplication and Division

Practice 1   Multiplying by a 1-Digit Number   41

Practice 2   Multiplying by a 2-Digit Number   45

Practice 3   Modeling Division with Regrouping   49

Practice 4   Dividing by a 1-Digit Number   55

Practice 5   Real-World Problems: Multiplication and Division   59

Math Journal: Reading and Writing Math   63

Put on Your Thinking Cap! Challenging Practice   65

Put on Your Thinking Cap! Problem Solving   66

4 Tables and Line Graphs

Practice 1   Making and Interpreting a Table   67

Practice 2   Using a Table   71

Practice 3   Line Graphs   75

Math Journal: Reading and Writing Math   79

Put on Your Thinking Cap! Challenging Practice   81

Put on Your Thinking Cap! Problem Solving   82

Cumulative Review for Chapters 3 and 4   83

Data and Probability

Practice 1   Average   93
Practice 2   Median, Mode, and Range   101
Practice 3   Stem-and-Leaf Plots   109
Practice 4   Outcomes   113
Practice 5   Probability as a Fraction   115
Practice 6   Real-World Problems: Data and Probability   119

Math Journal: Reading and Writing Math   132
Put on Your Thinking Cap! Challenging Practice   133
Put on Your Thinking Cap! Problem Solving   135

Fractions and Mixed Numbers

Practice 1   Adding Fractions   137
Practice 2   Subtracting Fractions   139
Practice 3   Mixed Numbers   141
Practice 4   Improper Fractions   147
Practice 5   Renaming Improper Fractions and
              Mixed Numbers   151
Practice 6   Renaming Whole Numbers when
              Adding and Subtracting Fractions   155
Practice 7   Fraction of a Set   157
Practice 8   Real-World Problems: Fractions   161

Math Journal: Reading and Writing Math   168
Put on Your Thinking Cap! Challenging Practice   169
Put on Your Thinking Cap! Problem Solving   170

Cumulative Review for Chapters 5 and 6   171

Mid-Year Review   181

BLANK

Name: _____   **Date:** _____

Place Value of Whole Numbers

Practice 1   Numbers to 100,000

Write each number in standard form.

> **Example**
> seventy-two thousand, four hundred sixty   *72,460*

1.   seventy thousand, eight hundred twenty-three   _____

2.   sixty-two thousand, four hundred eighteen   _____

3.   ninety-seven thousand, four hundred   _____

4.   thirty thousand, eleven   _____

Write each number in word form.

> **Example**
> 56,548   *fifty-six thousand, five hundred forty-eight*

5.   12,021   _____

6.   70,009   _____

7.   40,807   _____

Count on and fill in the blanks.

8.   81,000   82,000   83,000   _____   _____

9.   30,000   40,000   50,000   _____   _____

10.   10,000   15,000   20,000   _____   _____

Write the missing words and digits for each number.

> — *Example* —
>
> _____*two*_____ thousand, five _____*hundred*_____ twelve   2,51__2__

11.   sixty-one thousand, _____   ____1,001

12.   twenty-four _____, three hundred ten   24,3____0

13.   forty-five thousand, _____ hundred six   4____,206

14.   thirty-six thousand, one hundred _____   36,____89

Make each 5-digit number using all the cards. Do not begin a number with '0'.

5	7	2	0	9

15.   An odd number: _____

16.   An even number: _____

17.   A number with zero in the hundreds place: _____

18.   A number beginning with the greatest digit: _____

19.   A number with 2 in the tens place and 5 in the ones place: _____

20.   A number ending with 7: _____

Practice 2   Numbers to 100,000

Complete.

In 71,486,

> **Example**
>
> the digit 7 is in the _____ten thousands_____ place.

1.   the digit 1 is in the _____ place.

2.   the digit 4 is in the _____ place.

3.   the digit 8 is in the _____ place.

4.   the digit 6 is in the _____ place.

Find the value of each digit.

In 65,239,

> **Example**
>
> the digit 6 stands for _____60,000_____.

5.   the digit 5 stands for _____.

6.   the digit 2 stands for _____.

7.   the digit 3 stands for _____.

8.   the digit 9 stands for _____.

Write each number using the clues.

9.

> The value of the digit 1 is 100.
>
> The value of the digit 5 is 50.
>
> The value of the digit 3 is 3.
>
> The value of the digit 4 is 40,000.
>
> The value of the digit 2 is 2,000.

↓

The number is _____.

10.

> The digit 4 is in the hundreds place.
>
> The digit 2 is in the ten thousands place.
>
> The digit 9 is in the tens place.
>
> The digit 0 is in the ones place.
>
> The digit 5 is in the thousands place.

↓

The number is _____.

Write the missing numbers and words.

Example

In 36,172,

the digit 2 stands for ___2___ ones.

the digit 6 is in the __thousands__ place.

the digit in the ten thousands place is ___3___.

the value of the digit 7 is ___70___.

the digit ___1___ is in the hundreds place and its value is ___100___.

Write the missing numbers and words.

In 52,814,

11. the digit 4 stands for _____ ones.

12. the digit 1 is in the _____ place.

13. the digit in the ten thousands place is _____.

14. the value of the digit 8 is _____.

15. the digit _____ is in the thousands place and its value is _____.

Complete.

> **Example**
>
> 38,295 = ___3___ ten thousands + 8 thousands
>
> + 2 hundreds + 9 tens + 5 ones

16. 72,439 = 7 ten thousands + _____ thousands

+ 4 hundreds + 3 tens + 9 ones

17. 99,088 = 9 ten thousands + 9 thousands

+ _____ hundreds + 8 tens + 8 ones

Complete the expanded form.

18. 36,427 = 30,000 + _____ + 400 + 20 + 7

19. 17,503 = 10,000 + 7,000 + _____ + 3

20. 45,080 = 40,000 + _____ + 80

21. 20,000 + 6,000 + 20 + 5 = _____

22. 5 + 60 + 80,000 = _____

Solve.

23. Color the puzzle pieces that show the answers in Exercises 18 to 22.

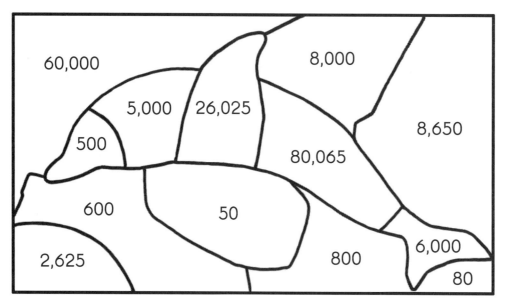

What is this picture?

_____

Practice 3   Comparing Numbers to 100,000

Write > or < in each ( ).

> *Example*
>
> 15,408 (>) 12,508
>
> | > means *greater than*.
> | < means *less than*.

1.   63,809 ( ) 36,908   **2.**   86,415 ( ) 86,591

3.   45,638 ( ) 8,594   **4.**   60,960 ( ) 69,999

Compare the eight numbers in Exercises 1 to 4.

5.   Which number is the greatest? _____

6.   Which number is the least? _____

Order these numbers.

> *Example*
>
> Begin with the least:
>
> | 52,081 | 63,456 | 51,125 |
>
> 51,125   52,081   63,456
>
> Begin with the greatest:
>
> | 76,332 | 74,236 | 81,152 |
>
> 81,152   76,332   74,236

Order these numbers.

7. Begin with the least:

97,136   79,631   96,137

_____

8. Begin with the greatest:

80,000   9,469   81,074

_____

Write the missing numbers.

Example

1,000 more than 82,586 is _____83,586_____.

_____17,312_____ is 40,000 less than 57,312.

9. 10,000 more than 56,821 is _____.

10. _____ is 50,000 less than 79,895.

11. 2,000 less than 18,563 is _____.

12. _____ is 3,000 more than 48,200.

Use the number line to count on or back.

Count on in steps of 4,000 from 20,000. Then write the number that you land on. The first one has been done for you.

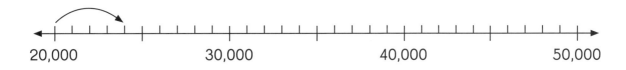

20,000   30,000   40,000   50,000

13.   1 step   24,000

I landed on 24,000 after 1 step.

14.   3 steps   ⬜

Count back in steps of 3,000 from 50,000. Then write the number that you land on.

15.   6 steps   ⬜

16.   8 steps   ⬜

Continue or complete the number patterns. Then write the rule for each pattern.

Example

39,580   49,580   59,580   _69,580_   _79,580_

Rule: _____Add 10,000._____

17.   96,500   86,500   76,500   _____   _____

Rule: _____

18.   39,860   _____   41,860   _____   43,860

Rule: _____

19.   25,000   20,000   15,000   _____   _____

Rule: _____

20.   _____   10,349   10,849   _____   _____   12,349

Rule: _____

21.   93,308   94,313   95,318   _____   _____

Rule: _____

22.   85,765   87,775   89,985   91,995   _____

Rule: _____

Math Journal

1. Kim wrote these statements about the three numbers shown here.
Do you agree? Explain why or why not.

3,869 is less than 85,945.

85,691 is greater than 85,945.

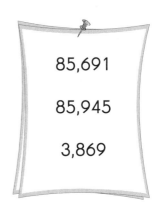

85,691

85,945

3,869

_____

_____

_____

_____

2. Sam continued this number pattern.
Do you agree? Explain why or why not.

5,400   10,400   10,600   15,600   15,800   (20,800)

_____

_____

_____

_____

3. Read the example. Then write your own 5-digit number and clues. Ask a friend or family member to solve your puzzle.

> *Example*
>
> **45,870**
>
> The digit 5 is in the thousands place.
>
> The value of the digit 7 is 70.
>
> The digit in the hundreds place is $10 - 2$.
>
> The digit in the ten thousands place is 1 less than the digit in the thousands place.
>
> The digit in the ones place is 0.

Number: _____

Clues: _____

_____

_____

_____

_____

Name: _____   **Date:** _____

Put On Your Thinking Cap!

Challenging Practice

Complete.

A 5-digit number is made up of different digits that are all odd numbers.

1.   What is the greatest possible number? _____

2.   What is the value of the digit in the hundreds place? _____

Continue the pattern.

3.   412   427   442   457   472   _____   _____

Fill in the blanks.

4.   What is 3 ten thousands + 14 tens + 16 ones? _____

5.   7 thousands = _____ hundreds 10 tens

Answer these questions.

In 7 ⑤, 8 [5] 9,

6.   what is the value of the digit 5 in the ◯ ? _____

7.   what is the value of the digit 5 in the ▢ ? _____

8.   what is the difference between the answers in **Exercises 6 and 7**? _____

9.   In 5 ◯, 2 [7] 8, the difference between the values of the digits in the ◯

and the ▢ is 8,930. What is the digit in the ◯ ? _____

Problem Solving

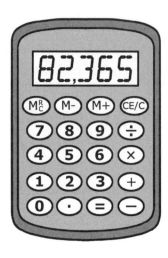

The ② button and the ⑥ button do not work.

Justin wants to enter the number 82,365.

Explain what he can do to key in the number. Give two solutions.

Use addition or subtraction to enter numbers of the right value.

_____

_____

_____

Chapter 2 Estimation and Number Theory

Practice 1 Estimation

Find each sum or difference. Then use rounding to check that your answers are reasonable. Round each number to the nearest hundred.

Example

534 + 287

534 + 287 = 821

Number	Rounded to the Nearest 100
534	500
287	300

The estimated sum rounded to the nearest 100 is 800.

Add: 500 + 300 = 800

821 is close to 800.
So, the answer is reasonable.

---

1. 515 + 342

2. 681 − 519

3. 170 + 725 + 333

4. 2,979 − 814

Find each sum or difference. Then use front-end estimation to check that your answers are reasonable.

Example

8,630 − 3,113

8,630 − 3,113 = 5,517

The answer is 5,517.

$$\text{⑧,630} − \text{③,113}$$
$$\downarrow \qquad \downarrow$$
$$8,000 − 3,000 = 5,000$$

8,630 − 3,113 is about 5,000.
5,517 is close to 5,000.
So, the answer is reasonable.

Estimate to check that the answer is reasonable.

---

5.   7,930 + 2,517

6.   3,166 − 1,625

7.   36,053 + 11,832

8.   9,705 − 8,250

Find each product. Then use rounding to check that your answers are reasonable. Round the 3-digit number to the nearest hundred.

Example

192 × 3

192 × 3 = 576

The answer is 576.

Number	Rounded to the Nearest 100 × 3
192	200 × 3 = 600

576 is close to 600.
So, the answer is reasonable.

The estimated product rounded to the nearest 100 is 600.

---

9.   233 × 4

10.   485 × 2

11.   117 × 5

12.   276 × 3

Find each product. Then use front-end estimation to check that your answers are reasonable.

Example

114 × 5

114 x 5 = 570

The answer is 570.

570 is close to 500. So, the answer is reasonable.

(1)14 x 5

↓

100 x 5 = 500

So, 114 x 5 is about 500.

The answer 570 is reasonable.

---

13.   108 × 3

14.   121 × 5

15.   439 × 2

16.   227 × 4

Find each quotient. Then use related multiplication facts to check that your answers are reasonable.

Example

85 ÷ 5

85 ÷ 5 = 17

The answer is 17.

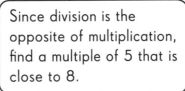

Since division is the opposite of multiplication, find a multiple of 5 that is close to 8.

5 x 10 = 50

5 x 20 = 100

85 is closer to 100 than to 50.
So, 85 ÷ 5 rounds to 100 ÷ 5.

100 ÷ 5 = 20
85 ÷ 5 is about 20.

17 is close to 20.
The answer 17 is reasonable.

---

17.   78 ÷ 2

18.   68 ÷ 4

19.   87 ÷ 3

20.   60 ÷ 5

Solve. Decide whether to find an estimate or an exact answer.

Example

Danny and his 3 friends buy baseball tickets for $26 each. About how much money do they need altogether?

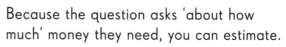

Because the question asks 'about how much' money they need, you can estimate.

4 x $30 = $120

They need about $120.

---

21. Jonathan, Shia, and Casey bought 35 toy figures. Each of the boys decides to make a team of 11 figures. Do they have enough toy figures?

22. A turtle hatchery collected 457 turtle eggs in a week. The next week, it collected 656 eggs. About how many eggs did the hatchery collect in the two weeks?

23. The table shows the number of beads in Stella's collection.

Color of Beads	Number
Blue	314
Yellow	417
Green	609

Stella needs 400 yellow beads, and 700 green beads to make a necklace. Does she have enough beads for the necklace?

Practice 2   Factors

Find the missing factors.

> *Example*
>
> 12 $1 \times \underline{\quad 12 \quad} = 12$
>
> $2 \times \underline{\quad 6 \quad} = 12$
>
> $3 \times \underline{\quad 4 \quad} = 12$
>
> The factors of 12 are
>
> 1, 2, 3, $\underline{\quad 4 \quad}$, $\underline{\quad 6 \quad}$, and $\underline{\quad 12 \quad}$.

1.   70 $1 \times \underline{\qquad} = 70$

$2 \times \underline{\qquad} = 70$

$5 \times \underline{\qquad} = 70$

$7 \times \underline{\qquad} = 70$

The factors of 70 are 1, 2, 5, 7, _____, _____,

_____, and _____.

Find the factors of each number.

2.   40

The factors of 40 are

_____.

3.   63

The factors of 63 are

_____.

Divide. Then answer each question.

4.   65 ÷ 5 = _____

Is 5 a factor of 65? _____

5.   46 ÷ 4 = _____

Is 4 a factor of 46? _____

Find the common factors of each pair of numbers.

		Factors	Common Factors
6.	10		
	15		
7.	24		
	36		

Divide. Then answer each question.

8.   18 ÷ 4 = _____   16 ÷ 4 = _____

Is 4 a common factor of 18 and 16? _____

9.   42 ÷ 3 = _____   84 ÷ 3 = _____

Is 3 a common factor of 42 and 84? _____

**Look at the numbers 80 , 27 , 40 , 62 , 36 , and 55 .
Then fill in the blanks.**

10.   Which of the numbers have 2 as a factor? _____

11.   Which of the numbers have 5 as a factor? _____

12.   Which of the numbers have both 2 and 5 as factors? _____

Name: _____ **Date:** _____

Each set of numbers are all the factors of a number. Find each number.

	Factors	Number
13.	1, 2, 4, and 8	
14.	1, 2, 3, 4, 6, and 12	
15.	1, 2, 3, and 6	
16.	1, 2, 4, 8, and 16	

Find the greatest common factor of each pair of numbers.

Example

12 and 28

Method 1

The factors of 12 are 1, 2, 3, 4, 6, and 12.
The factors of 28 are 1, 2, 4, 7, 14, and 28.
The common factors of 12 and 28
are 1, 2, and 4.
The greatest common factor
of 12 and 28 is 4.

Method 2

$$
\begin{array}{r|l}
2 & 12, 28 \\
\hline
2 & 6, 14 \\
\hline
& 3, \ 7
\end{array}
$$

2 x 2 = 4
The greatest common factor
of 12 and 28 is 4.

3 and 7 have no common factor other than 1.

17.   16 and 30

_____

Find the greatest common factor of the numbers.

18. 21 and 54

_____

Find all the factors. Then list the prime numbers.

> _Example_
>
> 13
>
> The factors of 13 are 1 and 13.
> 13 is a prime number.
>
> A prime number has only 2 factors, 1 and itself.

19. 12 _____

20. 7 _____

21. 19 _____

22. 24 _____

23. 11 _____

24. 63 _____

25. Look at the given numbers in **Exercises 19–24**.

The prime numbers are _____.

Explain your reasoning. _____

_____

Find all the factors. Then list the composite numbers.

> *Example*
>
> 18
>
> The factors of 18 are 1, 2, 3, 6, 9, and 18.
> 18 is a composite number.
>
> 18 has factors other than 1 and itself, so it is a composite number.

26. 20 _____ **27.** 15 _____

28. 5 _____ **29.** 17 _____

30. 33 _____ **31.** 27 _____

32. Look at the given numbers in **Exercises 26–31**.

The composite numbers are _____.

Explain your reasoning. _____

_____

Use the method given below to find prime numbers.

33.   Find the prime numbers between 1 and 50.

①	2	3	4	5	6	7	8	9	10
11	12	13	14	15	16	17	18	19	20
21	22	23	24	25	26	27	28	29	30
31	32	33	34	35	36	37	38	39	40
41	42	43	44	45	46	47	48	49	50

Step 1

1 is neither prime nor composite. So, 1 has been circled.
As 2 is the first prime number, it has been underlined.
Next, cross out all the numbers that can be divided by 2.

Step 2

3 is the next prime number. Underline it.
Then, cross out all the numbers that can be divided by 3.

Keep underlining the prime numbers and crossing out the numbers that can be divided by the prime numbers until you reach 50.

The prime numbers are _____

_____.

34.   Find two prime numbers between 60 and 90. _____

35.   Find two composite numbers between 60 and 90. _____

36.   Are there more prime numbers from 1 to 25 or from 26 to 50?

_____

_____

© Marshall Cavendish International (Singapore) Private Limited.

Name: _____ Date: _____

Practice 3 Multiples

Fill in the table with the multiples of each given number.

Example

Number	First Multiple	Second Multiple	Third Multiple	Fourth Multiple	Fifth Multiple
4	4	8	12	16	20

4, 8, 12, 16, and 20 are
multiples of 4.

To find a multiple of a number, multiply it by whole numbers starting from 1.

	Number	First Multiple	Second Multiple	Third Multiple	Fourth Multiple	Fifth Multiple
1.	7					
2.	8					
3.	9					

Fill in the blanks.

4. The first multiple of 9 is _____.

5. The second multiple of 8 is _____.

6. The first twelve multiples of 7 are _____

_____.

7. The seventh multiple of 7 is _____.

8. The twelfth multiple of 7 is _____.

Check (✓) the correct box and fill in the blank when necessary.

9. Is 32 a multiple of 6?

☐ Yes, it is the _____ multiple of 6.

☐ No, it is not a multiple of 6.

10. Is 63 a multiple of 9?

☐ Yes, it is the _____ multiple of 9.

☐ No, it is not a multiple of 9.

Use the numbers in the boxes to make your lists.

| 30 | 84 | 15 | 63 | 56 | 24 |

11. Multiples of 3 _____   **12.** Multiples of 8 _____

Each shaded area shows some of the multiples of a number.
Write the number in the box to the left of each shaded area.

13.

10   2

4   8   6

14.

27   9

15   81   18

15.

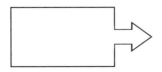

14   49

28   63   21

Find the common multiples and the least common multiple.

─ *Example* ─

$1 \times 2 = 2$ $1 \times 3 = 3$
$2 \times 2 = 4$ $2 \times 3 = 6$
$3 \times 2 = 6$ $3 \times 3 = 9$
$4 \times 2 = 8$ $4 \times 3 = 12$
$5 \times 2 = 10$ $5 \times 3 = 15$
$6 \times 2 = 12$ $6 \times 3 = 18$
$7 \times 2 = 14$
$8 \times 2 = 16$
$9 \times 2 = 18$

A common multiple is shared by two or more numbers.

A common multiple that is less than all the others is called the least common multiple.

The multiples of 2 are 2, 4, ⑥, 8, 10, ⑫, 14, 16, ⑱...

The multiples of 3 are 3, ⑥, 9, ⑫, 15, ⑱...

The first three common multiples of 2 and 3 are 6, 12, and 18 .

The least common multiple of 2 and 3 is 6 .

16. The first 14 multiples of 5 are 5, 10, 15, 20, 25, 30, 35, _____

_____.

The first 10 multiples of 7 are 7, 14, 21, 28, 35, 42, _____.

The first two common multiples of 5 and 7 are _____.

The least common multiple of 5 and 7 is _____.

17. The first 15 multiples of 4 are _____

_____.

The first 12 multiples of 5 are _____

_____.

The first three common multiples of 4 and 5 are _____.

The least common multiple of 4 and 5 is _____.

Write the first ten multiples of each number. Then find the least common multiple.

18.   8 and 5

8 _____

5 _____

The least common multiple of 8 and 5 is _____.

19.   6 and 9

6 _____

9 _____

The least common multiple of 6 and 9 is _____.

20.   12 and 15

12 _____

15 _____

The least common multiple of 12 and 15 is _____.

Fill in the blanks. More than one answer is possible.

21.   12 is the least common multiple of 3 and _____.

22.   32 is the least common multiple of 8 and _____.

23.   24 is the least common multiple of 6 and _____.

24.   15 is the least common multiple of 3 and _____.

25.   60 is the least common multiple of 15 and _____.

Put On Your Thinking Cap!

Challenging Practice

1. The estimated difference between two numbers is 60. Find two numbers that when rounded to the nearest ten, have a difference of 60. Use the numbers in the box.

135	128	61	141	74	56

2. When a 3-digit number is divided by a 1-digit number, the estimated quotient is 50. Think of two possible numbers that can give this quotient. Then check if your answer is correct.

3. A given number is a multiple of 4. It is between 6 and 15. It is a factor of 16. What is the number?

4. When a 3-digit number is rounded to the nearest ten and to the nearest hundred, the answer is the same. What is one possible number that fits this rule?

5. The number of bagels sold each day in two stores follows a pattern. Complete the table below to show this pattern.

Bagels Sold in Two Stores

	First Day	Second Day	Third Day	Fourth Day	Fifth Day	Sixth Day	Seventh Day
Store A	3	6		12			21
Store B	4	8		20			

Fill in the blanks using the data from the table above.

a. How many bagels did Store B sell on the seventh day? _____

b. The two stores sold the same number of bagels on different days. Which were the days?

Store A: _____   Store B: _____

Put On Your Thinking Cap!

Problem Solving

1. Mr. Chan bought some pencils for a group of students.
   If he gives them 2 pencils each, he will have 10 pencils left.
   If he gives them 3 pencils each, he will have none left.
   How many students are in the group?

2. On the opening day at a toy store, every third customer gets a ball
   and every fourth customer gets a stuffed animal. Sixty people come to
   the store. How many get both a ball and a stuffed animal?

3.   A square table can seat 4 people.
How many square tables are needed to seat 26 people if the tables are put together?

Hint: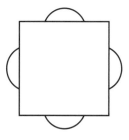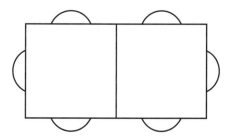

1 table can seat 4 people.   2 tables can seat 6 people.

Cumulative Review

for Chapters 1 and 2

Concepts and Skills

Write each number in standard form. *(Lesson 1.1)*

1. forty-eight thousand, six   _____

2. one hundred thousand   _____

3. sixty-nine thousand, two hundred eleven   _____

Write each number in word form. *(Lesson 1.1)*

4. 53,900 _____

5. 16,658 _____

6. 20,306 _____

Fill in the blank to write the number in expanded form. *(Lesson 1.1)*

7. $13,901 = 10,000 + \underline{\hspace{2cm}} + 900 + 1$

Fill in the blanks. *(Lesson 1.2)*

8. 100 more than 26,542 is _____.

9. _____ is 100 less than 79,023.

Circle the number that is greater. *(Lesson 1.2)*

10. 12,630 or 6,238

11. 45,200 or 45,496

12. 62,529 or 69,522

13. 90,236 or 87,415

Circle the number that is less. *(Lesson 1.2)*

14. 6,563 or 48,200

15. 67,186 or 67,254

16. 74,258 or 71,852

17. 96,125 or 69,521

Write the set of numbers in order from least to greatest. *(Lesson 1.2)*

18. 8,654   56,207   68,543   56,719

_____   _____   _____   _____

Continue or complete each number pattern. *(Lesson 1.2)*

19. 11,500   11,000   10,500   _____   _____

20. 63,800   64,100   64,400   _____   _____

21. 27,852   29,853   _____   33,855   35,856

Find each sum or difference. Then use rounding to check that your answers are reasonable. *(Lesson 2.1)*

22. 522 − 389

23. 456 + 790

Find each sum or difference. Then use front-end estimation to check that your answers are reasonable. *(Lesson 2.1)*

24. 432 + 759

25. 816 − 532

Find each product. Then use rounding to check that your answers are reasonable. *(Lesson 2.1)*

26. 383 × 2

27. 241 × 4

Find each product. Then use front-end estimation to check that your answers are reasonable. *(Lesson 2.1)*

28. 308 × 3

29. 126 × 5

Find each quotient. Then use related multiplication facts to check that your answers are reasonable. (Lesson 2.1)

30.   92 ÷ 4

31.   78 ÷ 3

Find the factors of each number. (Lesson 2.2)

32.   36 _____

33.   40 _____

34.   96 _____

Find the common factors of each pair of numbers. (Lesson 2.2)

35.   36 and 40

_____

36.   40 and 96

_____

Find the greatest common factor of each pair of numbers. (Lesson 2.2)

37.   30 and 16

_____

38.   48 and 18

_____

Find the prime and composite numbers. (Lesson 2.2)

| 47 | 31 | 92 | 63 | 57 | 135 |

39. The prime numbers are _____.

40. The composite numbers are _____.

List the first eight multiples of each number. (Lesson 2.3)

41. 4 _____

42. 6 _____

43. 9 _____

Find the first two common multiples of each pair of numbers. (Lesson 2.3)

44. 4 and 6

_____

45. 6 and 9

_____

Find the least common multiple of each pair of numbers. (Lesson 2.3)

46. 8 and 12

_____

47. 27 and 36

_____

Problem Solving

Solve. Show your work.

48. Make a 5-digit number using these clues.
The digit in the thousands place is 5.
The value of the digit in the ten thousands place is 20,000.
The digit in the tens place is 8.
One of the digits is a 0 and it is next to the digit 8.
The digit in the ones place is 2 less than the digit in the tens place.

The number is ⬜⬜,⬜⬜⬜.

49. 3,219 milliliters of water and 185 milliliters of orange syrup are mixed to make orange juice. About how much orange juice will there be?

50. An empty parking lot has 300 spaces.
215 cars and 89 SUVs drive into the parking lot.
How many vehicles do not have parking spaces?

51. Find a 2-digit number less than 50 using these clues.
It can be divided by 4 exactly.
When 4 is added to it, it can be divided by 5 exactly.

The number is _____.

52. Finch divides 12 peaches and 18 nectarines into the same number of equal groups. How many possible groups of each fruit can he make? How many are in each group?

Chapter 3 Whole Number Multiplication and Division

Practice 1 Multiplying by a 1-Digit Number

Multiply 962 by 6 and find the missing numbers.

Example

Step 1	2 ones × 6 = __12__ ones	$\begin{array}{r} 2 \\ \times\ 6 \\ \hline 1\ 2 \end{array}$
	= __1__ ten __2__ ones	

1. | Step 2 | 6 tens × 6 = _____ tens | $\begin{array}{r} 6\ 0 \\ \times\ \ \ 6 \\ \hline \end{array}$ |
|---|---|---|
| | = _____ hundreds _____ tens | |

2. | Step 3 | 9 hundreds × 6 = _____ hundreds | $\begin{array}{r} 9\ 0\ 0 \\ \times\ \ \ \ \ 6 \\ \hline \end{array}$ |
|---|---|---|
| | = _____ thousands _____ hundreds | |

3.

$$\begin{array}{r} 9\ \ 6\ \ 2 \\ \times\ \quad\quad\ 6 \\ \hline \end{array}$$

☐ ☐ ← 2 ones × 6

☐ ☐ ☐ ← 6 tens × 6

☐ , ☐ ☐ ☐ ← 9 hundreds × 6

☐ , ☐ ☐ ☐

Multiply 9,086 by 7 and find the missing numbers.

4. Step 1   6 ones × 7 = _____ ones

            = _____ tens _____ ones

$$\begin{array}{r} 6 \\ \times\ 7 \\ \hline \underline{} \end{array}$$

5. Step 2   _____ tens × 7 = _____ tens

            = _____ hundreds _____ tens

$$\begin{array}{r} \boxed{}\,0 \\ \times\ \ \ 7 \\ \hline \underline{} \end{array}$$

6. Step 3   _____ hundreds × 7 = _____ hundreds

$$\begin{array}{r} \boxed{}\,0\,0 \\ \times\ \ \ \ \ 7 \\ \hline \underline{} \end{array}$$

7. Step 4   _____ thousands × 7 = _____ thousands

            = _____ ten thousands _____ thousands

$$\begin{array}{r} \boxed{},0\,0\,0 \\ \times\ \ \ \ \ \ \ \ 7 \\ \hline \underline{} \end{array}$$

8.

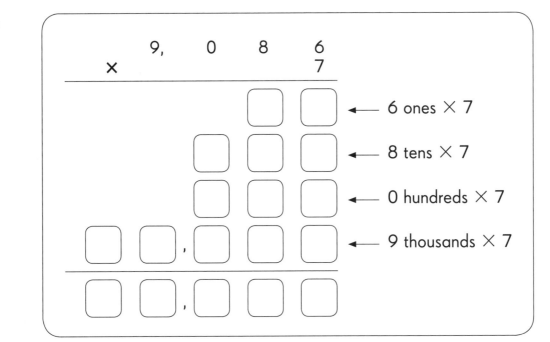

© Marshall Cavendish International (Singapore) Private Limited.

Multiply.

Example

		9	1	2
×				3

2 , 7 3 6

9.

		6	0	5
×				5

◻ , ◻ ◻ ◻

10.

	2,	1	3	4
×				6

◻ ◻ , ◻ ◻ ◻

11.

	6,	9	2	0
×				4

◻ ◻ , ◻ ◻ ◻

12.

	2,	0	1	9
×				7

◻ ◻ , ◻ ◻ ◻

13.

	1,	4	7	4
×				6

◻ , ◻ ◻ ◻

14.

	8,	5	7	2
×				8

◻ ◻ , ◻ ◻ ◻

15.

	6,	0	0	3
×				9

◻ ◻ , ◻ ◻ ◻

Find each product. Then solve the riddle.

> *Example*
>
> $425 \times 6 = \underline{\quad 2,550 \quad}$ (v)

16. $964 \times 8 = \underline{\hspace{2cm}}$ (a)   **17.** $682 \times 5 = \underline{\hspace{2cm}}$ (r)

18. $1,685 \times 3 = \underline{\hspace{2cm}}$ (w)   **19.** $1,936 \times 4 = \underline{\hspace{2cm}}$ (d)

20. $3,270 \times 3 = \underline{\hspace{2cm}}$ (e)

How do you say good-bye to the ocean?
Match the letters to the answers below to find out.

You $\underline{\hspace{2cm}}$ $\underline{\hspace{2cm}}$ $\underline{\overset{v}{\hspace{2cm}}}$ $\underline{\hspace{2cm}}$.

      5,055   7,712   2,550   9,810

Practice 2 Multiplying by a 2-Digit Number

Write the missing numbers. Then solve the riddle.

Example

15 × 10 = _____**150**_____ (r)   63 × 10 = _____**630**_____ (e)

1. 5 × 60 = 5 × _____ tens

= _____ tens

= _____ (n)

2. 16 × 20 = 16 × _____ tens

= _____ tens

= _____ (i)

3. 33 × 40 = 33 × _____ tens

= _____ tens

= _____ (l)

4. 29 × 30 = 29 × _____ tens

= _____ tens

= _____ (u)

5. 41 × 60 = 41 × _____ × 10

= _____ × 10

= _____ (B)

6. 96 × 40 = 96 × _____ × 4

= _____ × 4

= _____ (j)

7. 618 × 50

= 618 × _____ × 10

= _____ × 10

= _____ (o)

8. 752 × 70

= 752 × _____ × 7

= _____ × 7

= _____ (d)

What is the French word that has the same meaning as 'hello'?
Match the letters to the products below to find out.

___ ___ ___ ___ ___ ___ ___
2,460 30,900 300 3,840 30,900 870 150

Find each product.

9.   42 × 10 = _____

10.   786 × 10 = _____

11.   16 × 5 = _____

          16 × 50 = _____

12.   137 × 6 = _____

          137 × 60 = _____

13.   23 × 4 = _____

          23 × 40 = _____

14.   405 × 9 = _____

          405 × 90 = _____

Find each product.

15.   70 × 800

               7 × 8 = _____

               7 × 80 = _____

               7 × 800 = _____

     So, 70 × 800 = _____.

16.   300 × 90

           _____

           _____

           _____

           _____

Multiply. Find the missing numbers.

Example

```
          6   7
    ×     3   5
   ─────────────────
     [3] [3] [5]
  [2], [0] [1] [0]
   ─────────────────
  [2], [3] [4] [5]
```

17.

```
          6   1
    ×     8   6
   ─────────────────
     [ ] [ ] [ ]
  [ ], [ ] [ ] [ ]
   ─────────────────
  [ ], [ ] [ ] [ ]
```

18.

```
       8   7   2
    ×  6   2
   ──────────────────────
   [ ], [ ] [ ] [ ]
   [ ] [ ], [ ] [ ] [ ]
   ──────────────────────
   [ ] [ ], [ ] [ ] [ ]
```

19.

```
       7   0   9
    ×  4   9
   ──────────────────────
   [ ], [ ] [ ] [ ]
   [ ] [ ], [ ] [ ] [ ]
   ──────────────────────
   [ ] [ ], [ ] [ ] [ ]
```

Estimate each product. Round each number to its greatest place value.

Example

67 × 35 is about __70__ × __40__.

__70__ × __40__ = 2,800

20. 61 × 86 is about _____ × _____.

_____ × _____ = _____

21. 872 × 62 is about _____ × _____.

_____ × _____ = _____

22. 709 × 49 is about _____ × _____.

_____ × _____ = _____

Multiply. Then estimate to check that your answers are reasonable. Round each number to its greatest place value.

> **Example**
>
> $14 \times 18 = \underline{252}$
>
> $$\begin{array}{r} 14 \\ \times\ 18 \\ \hline 112 \\ 140 \\ \hline 252 \end{array}$$
>
> 14 is about 10.
> 18 is about 20.
>
> Estimate:
> $10 \times 20 = 200$
>
> 252 is close to 200. So, the answer is reasonable.

23. $48 \times 21 = \underline{\hspace{1.5cm}}$ **24.** $196 \times 34 = \underline{\hspace{1.5cm}}$

25. $608 \times 73 = \underline{\hspace{1.5cm}}$ **26.** $721 \times 54 = \underline{\hspace{1.5cm}}$

Practice 3 Modeling Division with Regrouping

Lisa cannot remember the steps to divide.
Help her complete the steps.

1.

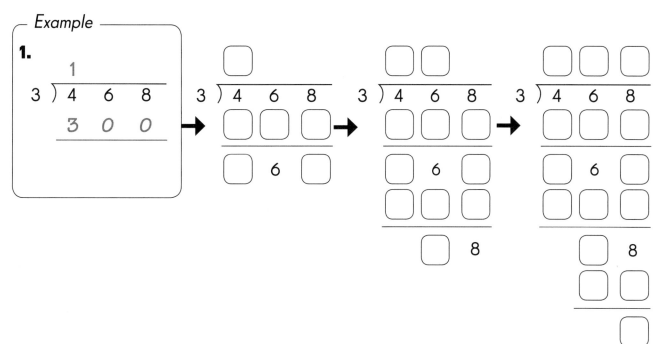

Example

2.

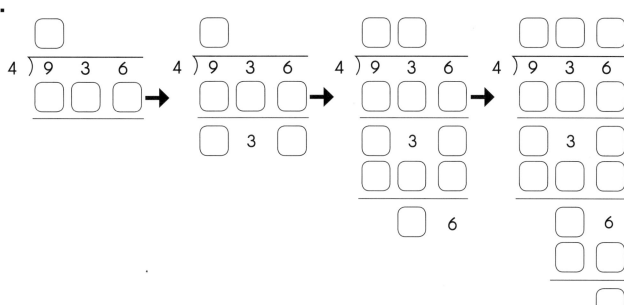

Divide. Then use the quotients to complete the number puzzle.

Down

3. $2 \overline{)7\ 9\ 8}$　　**4.** $3 \overline{)8\ 4\ 9}$　　**5.** $4 \overline{)6\ 9\ 6}$

Across

6. $5 \overline{)6\ 9\ 5}$　　**7.** $2 \overline{)7\ 5\ 4}$　　**8.** $4 \overline{)3\ 7\ 2}$

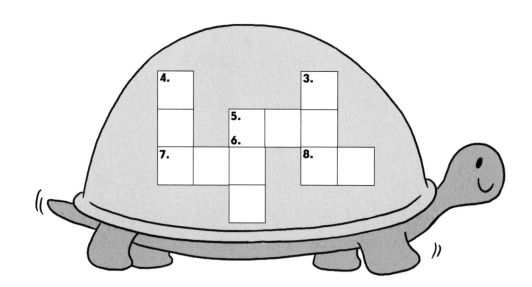

Divide. Then solve the riddle.

9.

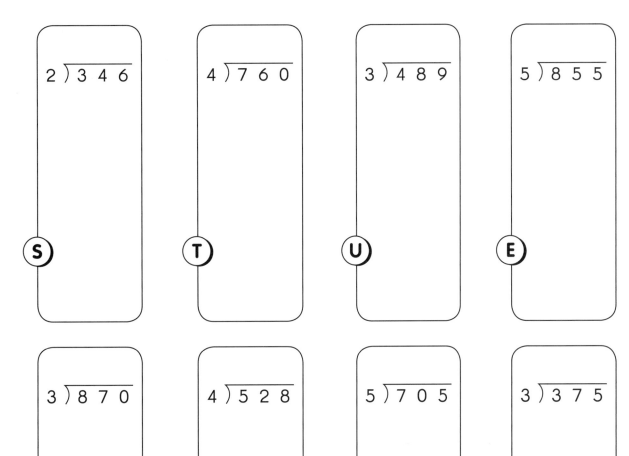

$2\overline{)346}$ **S**

$4\overline{)760}$ **T**

$3\overline{)489}$ **U**

$5\overline{)855}$ **E**

$3\overline{)870}$ **M**

$4\overline{)528}$ **P**

$5\overline{)705}$ **K**

$3\overline{)375}$ **R**

Which pet makes the loudest noise?
Match the letters to the quotients below to find out.

_____ _____ _____ _____ _____ _____ _____
190   125   163   290   132   171   190

Divide.

10. $516 \div 2 =$ _____

11. $144 \div 3 =$ _____

12. $396 \div 4 =$ _____

13. $885 \div 5 =$ _____

Look at the steps for dividing a 3-digit number by a 1-digit number.

Example

This shows the steps in division.

Step 1	Step 2	Step 3	Step 4	Step 5

Step 1:
```
     1
5)6  9  5
 5 [0][0]
     1
```

Step 2:
```
     1
5)6  9  5
 5 [0][0]
   1  9 [5]
```

Step 3:
```
     1  3
5)6  9  5
 5 [0][0]
   1  9 [5]
   1  5 [0]
        4
```

Step 4:
```
     1  3
5)6  9  5
 5 [0][0]
   1  9 [5]
   1  5 [0]
      4  5
```

Step 5:
```
     1  3  9
5)6  9  5
 5 [0][0]
   1  9 [5]
   1  5 [0]
      4  5
      4  5
         0
```

Write a number for each instruction box to match the instruction with the correct step for division. The first one has been done for you.

Divide the hundreds by 5.
Step 1

Divide the ones by 5.
Step 5

Divide the tens by 5.
Step 3

Regroup the remaining hundreds. Add the tens and ones.
Step 2

Regroup the remaining tens. Add the ones.
Step 4

Complete the division.

14.

Step 1	Step 2	Step 3	Step 4	Step 5
4)7 5 2	4)7 5 2	4)7 5 2	4)7 5 2	4)7 5 2

Then write the steps, using the exercise on page 53 as a guide.

Step 1 _____

_____

Step 2 _____

_____

Step 3 _____

_____

Step 4 _____

_____

Step 5 _____

_____

Practice 4 Dividing by a 1-Digit Number

Fill in the blanks to find each quotient.

Example

4,900 ÷ 7 = ___*49*___ hundreds ÷ 7

= ___*7*___ hundreds

= ___*700*___

1.   6,000 ÷ 3 = _____ thousands ÷ 3

= _____ thousands

= _____

2.   8,000 ÷ 2 = _____ thousands ÷ 2

= _____ thousands

= _____

3.   2,400 ÷ 6 = _____ hundreds ÷ 6

= _____ hundreds

= _____

Estimate each quotient.

4.   64 ÷ 3 is about _____ ÷ 3   5.   448 ÷ 9 is about _____ ÷ 9

= _____   = _____

6.   763 ÷ 4 is about _____ ÷ 4   7.   127 ÷ 5 is about _____ ÷ 5

= _____   = _____

Divide and find the missing numbers.

Example

```
      2  1  3
   _____
3 ) 6  3  9
    6  0  0
   _____
       3  9
       3  0
   _____
          9
          9
   _____
          0
```

8.

```
      [ ][ ][ ]
   _____
9 ) 9  2  7
    [ ][ ][ ]
   _____
       2 [ ]
      [ ][ ]
   _____
      [ ][ ]
      [ ][ ]
   _____
         [ ]
```

9.

```
      [ ],[ ][ ]
   _____
2 ) 6, 4  8  0
    [ ],[ ][ ]
   _____
       4 [ ][ ]
      [ ][ ][ ]
   _____
          8 [ ]
         [ ][ ]
   _____
          0
         [ ]
         [ ]
```

10.

```
      [ ][ ][ ]
   _____
7 ) 2, 1  8  4
    [ ],[ ][ ][ ]
   _____
        [ ][ ]
        [ ][ ]
   _____
        [ ][ ]
        [ ][ ]
   _____
           [ ]
```

Divide. Then estimate to check that your answers are reasonable.

┌─ *Example* ──────────────────────┐

```
            6   9   9
    9 ) 6,  2   9   1
        5,  4   0   0
            8   9   1
            8   1   0
                8   1
                8   1
                    0
```

Estimate:

6,291 is about 6,300.

6,300 ÷ 9 = 700

└──────────────────────────────────┘

11. 4) 3, 6   2   0

Estimate:

_____

_____

12. 7) 2, 8   0   7

Estimate:

_____

_____

13. 6) 1, 8   4   2

Estimate:

_____

_____

Find each quotient. Then estimate to check that your answers are reasonable.

Example

$1,144 \div 9 = \underline{127} \text{ R } \underline{1}$

```
        1  2  7  R 1
9 ) 1,  1  4  4
        9  0  0
        2  4  4
        1  8  0
           6  4
           6  3
              1
```

Estimate: 1,144 ÷ 9 is
about 900 ÷ 9 = 100.
The answer 127 R 1 is
reasonable.

14. $6,514 \div 4 = \underline{\hspace{1cm}} \text{ R } \underline{\hspace{1cm}}$

15. $1,340 \div 7 = \underline{\hspace{1cm}} \text{ R } \underline{\hspace{1cm}}$

16. $9,346 \div 8 = \underline{\hspace{1cm}} \text{ R } \underline{\hspace{1cm}}$

Practice 5 Real-World Problems: Multiplication and Division

Solve. Show your work.

> *Example*
>
> A company has 4,059 people. Their names are listed in alphabetical order and then divided into groups of 5.
>
> How many groups of 5 names are there and how many names are left?
>
> 4,059 ÷ 5 = 811 R 4
> There are 811 groups of 5 names,
> and 4 names are left.
>
> If the number of men in the company is 600 times the number of names left, how many men are there in the company?
>
> 600 × 4 = 2,400
> There are 2,400 men in the company.

1. Factory A produces 326 sweaters in a day. Factory B produces 107 more sweaters a day than Factory A.

   a. How many sweaters does Factory B produce in a day?

   b. How many sweaters do the two factories produce in 68 days?

2. In her shop, Lee had a piece of fabric measuring 150 meters. A customer asked her to sew 10 cushion covers, each requiring 3 meters of fabric. Another customer bought 21 meters of the same fabric. How much fabric does Lee have left?

3. A bakery produces 3,000 loaves of bread.
The bread is delivered to 75 stores.
Of the 75 stores, 67 receive 2,000 loaves of bread altogether.
The remaining stores receive an equal number of loaves of bread.
How many loaves does each of the remaining stores receive?

Name: _____   **Date:** _____

4. Before lunch, Cindy packed 850 oranges, and Glen packed 470 fewer oranges than Cindy. Glen went home after lunch, but Cindy went back to work. That afternoon, Cindy packed 3 times as many oranges as Glen had packed in the morning.

a. How many oranges did Glen pack?

b. How many oranges did Cindy pack altogether?

c. Cindy packed the oranges in bags of 5.
How many bags of oranges did Cindy pack?

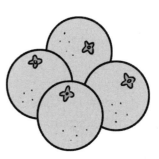

5. Ms. Edstrom had a budget of $1,500 to spend on a table and 6 chairs.
The total price was $249 under her budget amount.
The table cost 3 times as much as a chair.
What was the price of the table?

6. Kamala had 5,026 grams of flour in a canister. She bought a 4,157-gram bag of flour. She poured some flour from the bag to the canister. As a result, the mass of the flour in the canister is now twice the mass of the flour left in the bag. How much flour is in the bag now?

7. Mr. Shea saved $2,500 in April. His monthly salary is twice the amount he saved in April. In May, he saved a certain amount of money. He spent $4,200 more than the amount he saved. How much did he save in May?

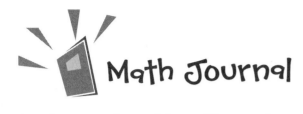 Math Journal

Look at each problem. Use estimation to explain why the answers are not reasonable.

> *Example*
>
> 5,268 × 8 = 2,144
>
> Explain.
>
> 5,268 is about 5,000 _____
>
> 5,000 x 8 = 40,000. _____
>
> So the answer is too small. _____

1.   725 × 6 = 700

Explain.

_____

_____

_____

2.   497 × 21 = 1,291

Explain.

_____

_____

_____

Use estimation to explain why the answer is not reasonable.

3. 6,021 ÷ 3 = 207

Explain.

_____

_____

_____

Solve. Show your work.

4. Look at the number sentence.

72 ÷ 6 = 12

How would you use this to find the missing quotient?

7,200 ÷ 6 = ☐

_____

_____

_____

Put On Your Thinking Cap!

 Challenging Practice

Charlie has 1,243 stamps. He gives away 12 stamps. His father gives him 415 stamps. He divides as many stamps as possible equally among 4 albums.

1. How many stamps did he place in each album?

2. Based on your answer in **Exercise 1**, how many stamps are left over?

 Put On Your Thinking Cap!

 Problem Solving

1. The cost of 2 televisions and 3 DVD players is $1,421.
The cost of 1 DVD player is half the cost of 1 television.
What is the cost of 1 television?

Chapter 4 Tables and Line Graphs

Practice 1 Making and Interpreting a Table

These are the vehicles that passed through a town center between 10:00 A.M. and 10:15 A.M. last Sunday.

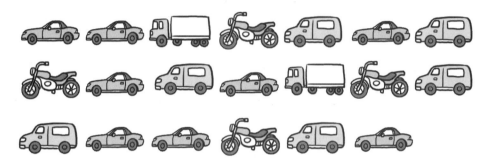

Make tally marks to count the number of each type of vehicle that passed through the town center.

Example

Number of cars _____ ~~||||~~ ||| _____

1. Number of motorcycles _____

2. Number of vans _____

3. Number of trucks _____

Tally marks are used to organize data in groups of 5.

Using the data above, complete the table.

4. **Vehicles that Passed Through the Town Center**

Type of Vehicle	Car	Motorcycle	Van	Truck
Number of Vehicles	8			

The school nurse keeps the health records of all the students. These cards show the height and weight of nine students.

Name: Pablo
Height: 62 in.
Weight: 114 lb

Name: Grant
Height: 59 in.
Weight: 110 lb

Name: Tamara
Height: 55 in.
Weight: 103 lb

Name: John
Height: 55 in.
Weight: 114 lb

Name: Mei Li
Height: 59 in.
Weight: 103 lb

Name: Pauline
Height: 62 in.
Weight: 92 lb

Name: Nita
Height: 55 in.
Weight: 103 lb

Name: Evan
Height: 51 in.
Weight: 84 lb

Name: Samantha
Height: 55 in.
Weight: 92 lb

Complete. Use the data on the cards.

5.

Height of Students

Height (in.)	Number of Students
51	
	4
	2
62	

Weight of Students

Weight (lb)	Number of Students
84	1
92	
	3
110	
	2

Jane used tally marks to record the number of pets adopted from an animal shelter in a week.

Pets Adopted from an Animal Shelter

Pet	Tally
Guinea Pigs	~~////~~ ////
Hamsters	~~////~~ ~~////~~ ~~////~~
White Mice	~~////~~ ~~////~~ ~~////~~ ///
Rabbits	~~////~~

Complete. Use the data in the tally chart.

6.   **Pets Adopted from an Animal Shelter**

Pet	Number of Pets Adopted
Guinea Pigs	
Hamsters	
White Mice	
Rabbits	

Complete. Use the data in the table.

7. _____ white mice were adopted.

8. _____ guinea pigs were adopted.

9. _____ more white mice than guinea pigs were adopted.

10. Three times as many _____ as _____ were adopted.

11. The pets that were adopted most often from the animal shelter were

_____.

Gary has a coin collection. The bar graph shows the number of coins he collected from different countries.

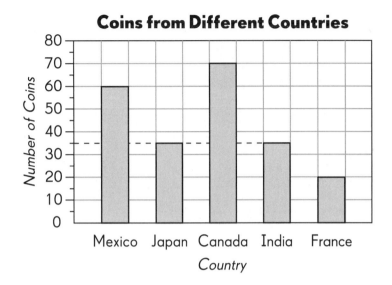

Coins from Different Countries

Use the data in the graph to complete the table. Then use the data in the table to complete the sentences.

12.   **Coins from Different Countries**

Country	Number of Coins
Mexico	
Japan	
Canada	
India	
France	

13. Gary has the same number of coins from _____ and _____.

14. Gary has half as many coins from Japan as he has from _____.

15. He has _____ more coins from Mexico than from India.

16. Gary gave away all his coins from Canada. He now has the greatest number

of coins from _____.

Practice 2   Using a Table

Use the data in the table to complete the sentences below.

The table shows pictures at rows, columns, and intersections.

	Column 1	Column 2	Column 3	Column 4	Column 5	Column 6
Row A		☆			🐟	
Row B			🏀			🍎
Row C		🌙				
Row D				🦟		
Row E	🍪					

Example

 _____ is at the intersection of Row B and Column 3.

 is in Row ____B____ and Column ____3____.

1. _____ is at the intersection of Row E and Column 1.

2. 🍎 is in Row _____ and Column _____.

3. ☆ is in Row _____ and Column _____.

4. 🦟 is in Row _____ and Column _____.

The table shows part of Bill's class schedule from Monday through Wednesday.

Bill's Schedule

Time	Monday	Tuesday	Wednesday
09:00 A.M. – 10:00 A.M.	Science	Math	History
10:00 A.M. – 11:00 A.M.	Math	Geography	Science
11:00 A.M. – 12:00 P.M.	English	Science	Math
12:00 P.M. – 1:00 P.M.	Lunch	Lunch	Lunch

Use the table to answer the questions.

5. What class does Bill have between 10:00 A.M. and 11:00 A.M. on

Mondays? _____

6. What class does Bill have between 9:00 A.M. and 10:00 A.M. on

Wednesdays? _____

7. His lunch break on Wednesday is between _____.

8. His Math class on _____ is between 11:00 A.M. and 12:00 P.M.

9. His Geography class on _____ is between 10:00 A.M. and 11:00 A.M.

Maria and Vinny collected stamps from three different countries: Singapore, Malaysia, and Thailand. The number of stamps collected is shown in the table below.

Stamps Collected

Collector	Singapore	Malaysia	Thailand
Maria	15		23
Vinny		18	
Total	46	60	52

Complete the table, and answer the questions.

10.   How many Thailand stamps did Vinny collect? _____

11.   How many Thailand stamps did Maria and Vinny collect

altogether? _____

12.   How many more Malaysia stamps than Singapore stamps did Maria and

Vinny collect altogether? _____

13.   Who collected more stamps: Maria or Vinny? _____

14.   How many stamps did they collect altogether? _____

The table shows the number of quarters and nickels that five students saved.

Quarters and Nickels Saved

| Name | Quarters (25¢) | | Nickels (5¢) | | Total Amount Saved ($) |
	Number of Coins Collected	Amount Saved ($)	Number of Coins Collected	Amount Saved ($)	
Amy	16		20		
Bernard	10		7		
Chin	18		25		
Dawn	21		9		
Ernest	15		15		

Complete the table, and answer the questions.

15. Who saved the greatest amount? _____

16. Who saved the least amount? _____

17. How many more coins did Chin collect than Ernest? _____

18. How much more must Bernard save in order to have the same amount

as Dawn? _____

19. Which two students saved a total of less than $7.50?

How much less ?

_____

20. Which two students collected the same number of coins?

_____

21. Of the two students in **Exercise 20**, who saved more money?

How much more?

_____

Practice 3   Line Graphs

Use the data in the line graphs to answer each question.

The line graph shows the change in Rodney's weight over a few years.

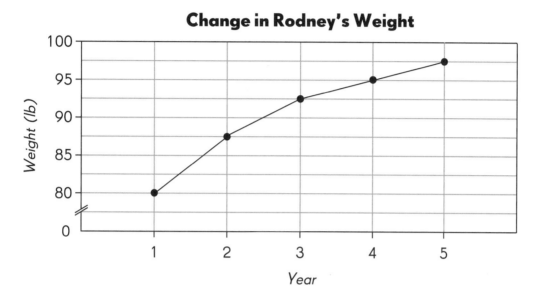

Change in Rodney's Weight

Example

What was Rodney's weight in the second year?

__87.5 lb__

In which year was the increase in Rodney's weight the

greatest? __Between the first and second year__

A line graph shows
how data changes
over time.

---

1.   What was Rodney's weight in the

    a.   fourth year? _____   **b.**   fifth year? _____

    c.   What was the increase in Rodney's weight between

       these two years? _____

2.   In which year was the increase in Rodney's weight 5 lb?

_____

The line graph shows the temperature of an object being heated over five hours.

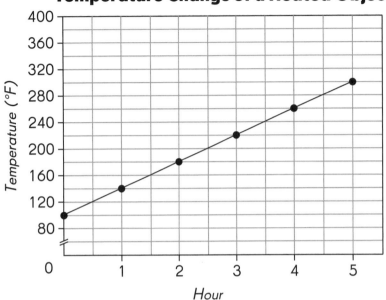

Temperature Change of a Heated Object

3. What was the temperature of the object in the second hour? _____

4. What was the temperature of the object in the fourth hour? _____

5. What was the increase in temperature between the second hour and the

fourth hour? _____

Use the data from the graph to complete the table.

Temperature Change of a Heated Object

6.

Time (h)	0	1	2	3	4	5
Temperature (°F)	100				260	

7. Did the temperature increase by the same amount every hour?

_____

The line graph shows the change in height while Ali was climbing a mountain.

Change in Height

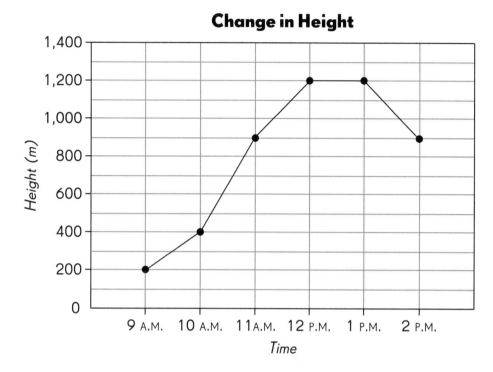

8. At what time was Ali at a height of 200 meters? _____

9. At what height was Ali at 2 P.M.? _____

10. During which hour was the increase in height the greatest?

_____

11. When did Ali take a break from climbing? _____

12. Explain what happened from 1 P.M. to 2 P.M.

_____

Choose an appropriate graph to display the data. Write *bar graph*, *line graph*, or *picture graph*. Explain your choice.

13. Anna recorded the rainfall amounts (in centimeters) in each month from January to June.

_____

_____

14. Jim organized a party for 20 of his friends. He recorded the number of friends who liked each flavor of ice-cream — vanilla, strawberry, and chocolate. 4 friends liked vanilla ice-cream, 8 friends liked strawberry ice-cream, and 8 friends liked chocolate ice-cream.

_____

_____

15. Temperature change of water (in °F) when it is heated over 20 minutes.

_____

_____

16. Level of water remaining in a leaking tank recorded over four hours.

_____

_____

© Marshall Cavendish International (Singapore) Private Limited.

Math Journal

Michael bought a new car in 2001 for $24,000. The line graph shows how the value of his car changed from 2001 to 2005.

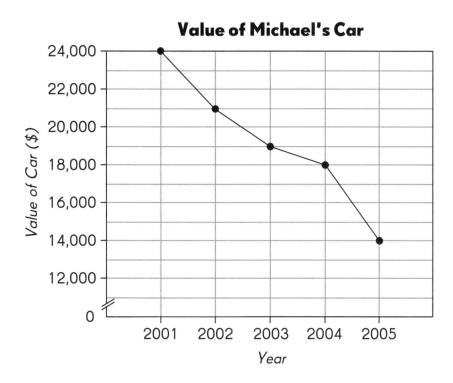

Value of Michael's Car

Write four questions that can be answered using the data in the line graph. Then write the answers.

a.   Question

_____

_____

Answer

_____

_____

b. Question

_____

_____

Answer

_____

_____

c. Question

_____

_____

Answer

_____

_____

d. Question

_____

_____

Answer

_____

_____

Put On Your Thinking Cap!

Challenging Practice

Look at the line graph.

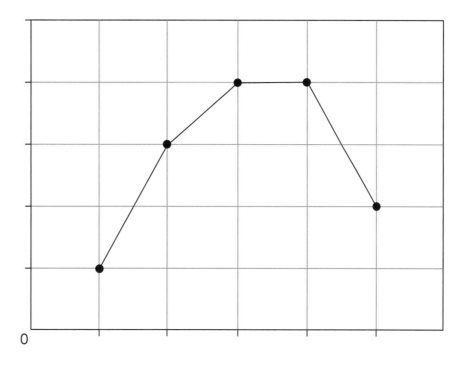

1. Suggest what data this graph could be showing.

_____

_____

2. Create a title, scale and labels for the graph. Show these on the graph.

3. Why do you think the line is horizontal from point 3 to point 4?

_____

_____

 **Put On Your Thinking Cap!**

 Problem Solving

The graph shows the number of guppies in a tank over a few months.

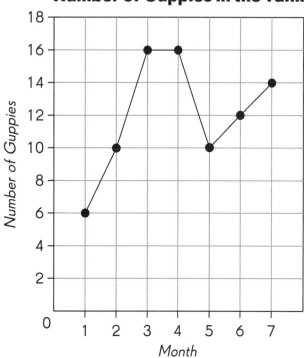

Number of Guppies in the Tank

Number of Guppies

Month

1. During which 1-month interval was the increase in the number of guppies the greatest? _____

2. How many guppies were moved to another tank between the fourth and the fifth month ?_____

3. How many guppies were added to the tank in the second month? _____

4. Why is the line horizontal from the third to the fourth month?

_____

_____

Cumulative Review

for Chapters 3 and 4

Concepts and Skills

Multiply. *(Lessons 3.1 and 3.2)*

1. $27 \times 8 =$ _____

2. $7,365 \times 9 =$ _____

3. $94 \times 67 =$ _____

4. $827 \times 61 =$ _____

5. $625 \times 29 =$ _____

6. $944 \times 38 =$ _____

Divide. *(Lessons 3.3 and 3.4)*

7. $216 \div 3 =$ _____   **8.** $432 \div 8 =$ _____

9. $5{,}520 \div 6 =$ _____   **10.** $2{,}828 \div 7 =$ _____

11. $5{,}398 \div 5 =$ _____   **12.** $7{,}436 \div 7 =$ _____

Name: _____ Date: _____

Study the bar graph and answer the questions. *(Lesson 4.1)*

The bar graph shows the number of times Will wrote the letters A, B, C, D, and E on a paper.

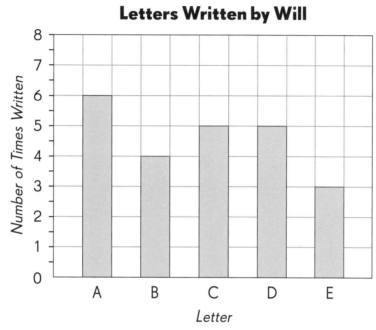

Letters Written by Will

Complete the table. Use the data in the graph.

13. **Letters Written by Will**

Letter	A		C		
Number of Times Written	6				

Complete. Use the data in the table.

14. Which letter did Will write the greatest number of times? _____

15. How many more letter 'A's did Will write than the letter he wrote the least number of times? _____

16. How many more letter 'A's must be written so that the number of letter 'A's will be 3 times the number of letter 'B's? _____

Count the buttons and complete the table. *(Lesson 4.1)*

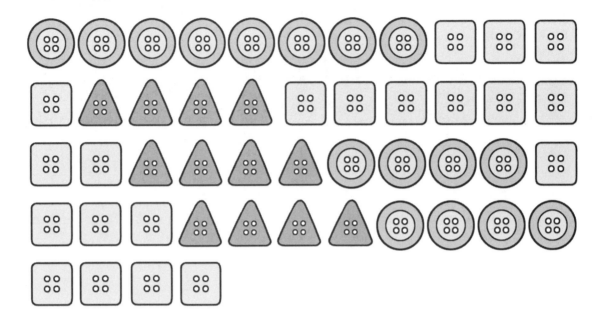

17.

Types of Buttons

Buttons	Number
Round Buttons	
Square Buttons	
Triangular Buttons	
Total	

Complete. Use the data in the table.

18. The least number of buttons are the _____ buttons.

19. There are _____ more square buttons than round buttons.

Complete the table by finding the rows, columns, and intersections. *(Lesson 4.2)*

The table shows the types of sandwiches ordered by a group of students at lunchtime.

20.

Sandwiches Ordered by Students

Types of Sandwiches	Boys	Girls	Total
Chicken	6	4	10
Roast Beef	12	18	
Tuna	7		15
Grilled Vegetables	3	18	21

Complete. Use the data in the table.

21. How many students ordered roast beef? _____

22. Find the number that should appear in the intersection for 'Tuna' and 'Girls'.

_____

23. In which column does the number '7' appear? _____

24. In which row does the number '6' appear? _____

25. The number '4' appears in the intersection of the column for _____

and the row for _____ .

Complete the table by finding the rows, columns, and intersections. *(Lesson 4.2)*

The table shows the 50-cent and 20-cent toys that three friends bought for party favors.

26.

Name	50-cent Toys		20-cent Toys		Total Cost
	Number	Cost	Number	Cost	
Ashin	5	$2.50	9	$1.80	
Benjamin	6		7		
Cara	4		8		

Complete. Use the data in the table.

27.   Who bought the most toys? _____

28.   Who spent the most on the toys? _____

29.   How much more did Benjamin spend than Cara? _____

30.   How much did they spend on 20-cent toys altogether? _____

31.   How much more did they spend on 50-cent toys than on

20-cent toys? _____

Complete. Use the data in the line graph. (Lesson 4.3)

The graph shows the amount of water in a leaking tank over 7 hours.

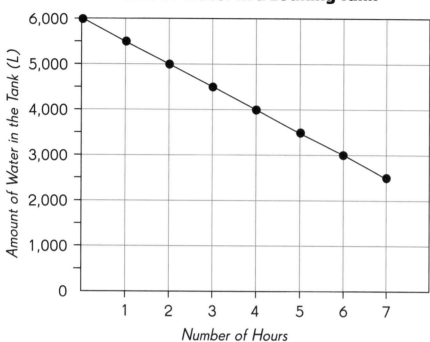

Amount of Water in a Leaking Tank

32.   What was the amount of water in the tank at the start? _____

33.   What was the amount of water in the tank after 7 hours? _____

34.   After how many hours was the amount of water in the tank

       half that at the start? _____

35.   The owner of the tank paid a fine of $1 for every 8 liters of

       water lost. How much would the fine be after 4 hours? _____

Complete. Use the data in the line graph. (Lesson 4.3)

The line graph shows the change in water level in a tank over 6 minutes.

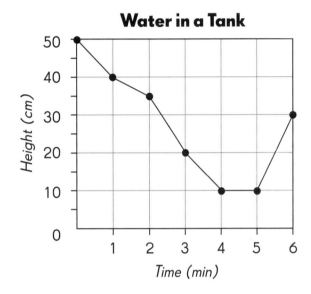

Water in a Tank

36. What was the height of the water after

    a.   2 minutes? _____   b. $3\frac{1}{2}$ minutes? _____

37. What was the decrease in the height of the water from the first to the

    second minute? _____

38. During which 1-minute interval did the water level decrease the most?

    From the _____ minute to the _____ minute.

39. During which 1-minute interval did the water level increase by 20 centimeters?

    From the _____ minute to the _____ minute.

40. Was the tank ever empty? _____

    If the tank were ever empty, how would you tell from the graph?

    _____

Problem Solving

Solve. Show your work.

41.   Mr. Suarez has $2,760 to buy family meals for the local food pantry.

  a.   What is the greatest number of family meals he can buy if each meal costs $9?

  b.   How much money would he have left after buying the meals?

42.   A grocer bought two bags of dried fruit. One bag contained 4,950 ounces of fruit and the other bag contained 2,730 ounces of fruit. He repacked the fruit equally into 8 smaller packets. What was the weight of the fruit in each packet?

43. A farmer packed 37 pumpkins. Each pumpkin had a weight of about 48 ounces. He put them into three baskets.

- The weight of the pumpkins in Basket A was 3 times that of the pumpkins in Basket C.
- The weight of the pumpkins in Basket B was twice that of the pumpkins in Basket C.
- The weight of the empty Basket C was 140 ounces.

What was the total weight of Basket C and the pumpkins in it?

44. The tank at a gas station contained 400 gallons of gas. A tanker truck that contained 8,100 gallons of gas filled the station's tank. After that the tanker truck had 4 times as much gas as the station's tank. How much gas did the tanker truck put into the station's tank?

Chapter 5 Data and Probability

Practice 1 Average

Find the mean or average of each set of data.

Example

6, 14, 18, 22

Step 1 Find the sum of the four numbers.

____6____ + ____14____ + ____18____ + ____22____ = ____60____

Step 2 Divide the sum by 4.

____60____ ÷ 4 = ____15____

The mean or average of the set of numbers is ____15____.

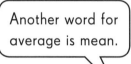

Another word for average is mean.

---

1. Here are the weights of 5 pieces of luggage at an airport.

14 lb, 18 lb, 21 lb, 27 lb, 30 lb

Step 1 Find the total weight of all the pieces of luggage.

_____ + _____ + _____ + _____ + _____

= _____ lb

Step 2 Divide the total by 5.

_____ ÷ 5 = _____ lb

What is the average weight of the pieces of luggage? _____ lb

Find the mean of each set of data.

2.   37, 0, 67, 44

3. $8, $12, $15, $29

4.   15 pt, 21 pt, 34 pt, 48 pt, 52 pt

5.   28 yd, 61 yd, 19 yd, 43 yd, 89 yd, 126 yd

6.   55 lb, 246 lb, 100 lb, 34 lb, 95 lb, 460 lb

Complete. Use the data in the table.

The table shows the distances Wayne jogged on 5 days.

Distances Wayne Jogged on Five Days

Day	Distance Jogged
Monday	3 km
Tuesday	2 km
Wednesday	4 km
Thursday	5 km
Friday	6 km

7. How many kilometers did he jog altogether?

8. On average, how many kilometers did he jog each day?

Complete. Use the data in the table.

The table shows the number of trophies a school collected over 6 years.

Trophies Collected Over Six Years

Year	Number of Trophies Collected
1	15
2	9
3	12
4	18
5	20
6	22

9. What is the total number of trophies collected in 6 years?

10. What is the average number of trophies collected each year?

Solve. Show your work.

Example

Mrs. Lim made 6,250 milliliters of orange juice and poured it into 5 containers. Find the mean amount of juice in each container.

6,250 ÷ 5 = 1,250 mL

The mean amount of juice in each container is 1,250 mL.

$$\text{Mean} = \frac{\text{Total number or amount}}{\text{Number of items}}$$

---

11. A chess club began accepting members on January 1.
By September 30 of the same year, the club had a total of
504 members. What was the average number of members who joined
the club each month?

Solve. Show your work.

Example

The average number of goals scored by a soccer team in a game was 4.
The team played a total of 22 games. What was the total number of goals
scored by the team?

4 × 22 = 88 goals

Total score	=	Average score	×	Number of games

The total number of goals scored by
the team was 88.

12. The mean length of the sides of a triangular plot of land is 18 yards.
What is its perimeter?

Solve. Show your work.

13. There are 12 peaches in a carton. The mean mass of all the peaches is 175 grams. What is their total mass?

14. Alicia sews costumes for a school play. She takes an average of 86 minutes to sew each costume. How long would she take to sew 16 of these costumes?

Practice 2   Median, Mode, and Range

Find the median, mode, and range.

Example

4, 6, 5, 6, 8, 8, 10, 8

Find the median.

4, 5, 6, (6, 8,) 8, 8, 10

Arrange the numbers in order from least to greatest. The middle number or the mean of the two middle numbers is the median.

Since there are two middle numbers, 6 and 8, find the mean of the two numbers.

The median of the data set is $\frac{6+8}{2} = \frac{14}{2} = 7$.

Find the mode.

4, 5, 6, 6, (8,) (8,) (8,) 10

The number that appears most often is the mode. There can be more than one mode. If all the numbers appear the same number of times, there is no mode.

The mode of the data set is 8.

Find the range.

4, 5, 6, 6, 8, 8, 8, 10

Range = 10 − 4

       = 6

The difference between the greatest and the least number is the range.

The range of the data set is 6.

Find the median, mode, and range of each set of data.

1.   50, 52, 58, 50, 47, 43, 52, 60, 49, 52

Median:

Mode:

Range:

2.   15 in., 18 in., 12 in., 14 in., 30 in., 15 in., 15 in.

Median:

Mode:

Range:

3.   9 lb, 11 lb, 14 lb, 20 lb, 14 lb, 20 lb, 14 lb, 20 lb

Median:

Mode:

Range:

Example

The line plot shows the number of words spelled correctly by each contestant in a spelling bee. Each X represents one contestant.

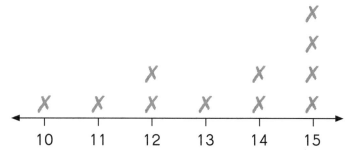

Number of Words Spelled Correctly

An X above 15 on the number line represents a contestant who spelled 15 words correctly.

Complete. Use the data in the line plot.

_____11_____ contestants took part in the spelling bee.

The median number of words spelled correctly is ____14____.

The number of contestants who spelled the greatest

number of words correctly is ____4____.

The mode of the set of data is ____15____ words.

The difference between the greatest and the least number of words spelled

correctly is ____5____.

Make a line plot to show the data.

The table shows the number of bull's eyes each player scored out of 10 shots in a dart competition.

Results of Dart Competition

Number of Bull's Eyes	5	6	7	8	9	10
Number of Players	1	2	3	4	0	1

Complete. Use the data in your line plot.

4. The median number of bull's eyes scored is _____.

5. There are _____ players altogether.

6. The number of bull's eyes that was scored the most is _____.

7. The range of the set of data is _____.

8. _____ players scored 7 bull's eyes, and the winner scored

_____ bull's eyes.

Complete the table based on the information given.

A number cube has six faces numbered 1 to 6. John tossed two number cubes several times and added the numbers each time.

Sum of the Number Cubes

Total	Tally	Number of Times
2	/	
3		
4	//	
5	/	
6	//	
7	////	
8	//	
9	/	
10		
11	/	
12		

Complete. Use the data in the table.

9. John threw the two number cubes _____ times altogether.

10. Make a line plot to show the total for each toss.

11. The median of the set of data is _____.

12. The mode of the set of data is _____.

13. The range of the set of data is _____.

Find the mean of each set of data.

Example

Haley made a line plot to show the number of points she scored in a computer math game over three weeks.

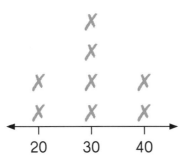

Number of Points Scored in Week 1

First, find the total number of points she scored.

20 points × _____2_____ times = _____40_____

30 points × _____4_____ times = _____120_____

40 points × _____2_____ times = _____80_____

Mean = $\dfrac{\text{Total number of points scored}}{\text{Number of times played}}$

$= \dfrac{40 + 120 + 80}{2 + 4 + 2} = \dfrac{240}{8} = 30$

Haley's mean score for each game in Week 1 is _____30_____ points.

14.

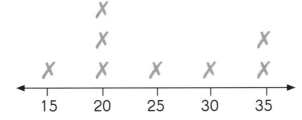

Number of Points Scored in Week 2

15 points × _____ time(s) = _____

20 points × _____ time(s) = _____

25 points × _____ time(s) = _____

30 points × _____ time(s) = _____

35 points × _____ time(s) = _____

Mean = _____

= _____ = _____

Haley's mean score for each game in Week 2 is _____ points.

Find the mean of the set of data.

15.

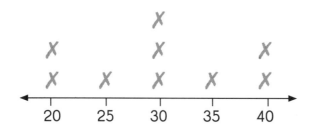

Number of Points Scored in Week 3

20 points ✗ _____ time(s) = _____

25 points ✗ _____ time(s) = _____

30 points ✗ _____ time(s) = _____

35 points ✗ _____ time(s) = _____

40 points ✗ _____ time(s) = _____

Mean = _____

       = _____

       = _____

Haley's mean score for each game in Week 3 is _____ points.

16. Compare the line plots for Weeks 2 and 3. Can you tell which data set has a greater mean just by looking at the line plots? What part of the line plot makes you think that?

Practice 3   Stem-and-Leaf Plots

Complete. Use the data in the stem-and-leaf plot.

— *Example* —

The stem-and-leaf plot shows 9 students' grades on a math test.

Math Test Scores	
Stem	**Leaves**
①︎	5
2	5 8
3	2 2 2 7
4	2 5

$$1 \mid 5 = 15$$

> In a stem-and-leaf plot, the leaves are the ones digits and the stems are the digits to the left of the ones digit.

The stem 3 has _____4_____ leaves.

The median, the middle score, is ____32____.

The mode, the most frequent score, is ____32____.

The range of the scores is ____30____.

The outlier, the number farthest from the others, is ____15____.

Complete. Use the data in the stem-and-leaf plot.

The stem-and-leaf plot shows the heights of 12 children in centimeters.

Heights of Children (cm)	
Stem	**Leaves**
9	6 8
10	4 6 6 6
11	0 3 3 5
12	4 9

9 | 6 = 96

1. The stem 12 has _____ leaves.

2. The height of the shortest child is _____ centimeters.

3. 10 | 4 stands for _____ centimeters, and 11 | 4 stands

for _____ centimeters.

4. The median height of the children is _____ centimeters.

5. The mode of the set of data is _____ centimeters.

6. The range of the heights is _____ centimeters.

Make a stem-and-leaf plot to show the data.

The table shows the points scored by a school team in eight basketball games one season.

Points Scored in Basketball Games

Game	1	2	3	4	5	6	7	8
Points Scored	50	62	60	68	60	72	56	76

Points Scored in Basketball Games	
Stem	**Leaves**

Complete. Use the data in the stem-and-leaf plot.

7. The stem 7 has _____ leaves.

8. The stem _____ has the greatest number of leaves.

9. The median number of points scored is _____.

10. The modal number of points scored is _____.

11. The range of the set of data is _____.

Make a stem-and-leaf plot to show the data.

Seven children weighed their dogs at a pet-care center.

15 lb, 12 lb, 17 lb, 15 lb, 21 lb, 17 lb, 15 lb

Weights of Dogs (lb)	
Stem	Leaves

Complete. Use the data in the stem-and-leaf plot.

12. The weight of the heaviest dog is _____ pounds.

13. The median weight of the dogs is _____ pounds.

14. The mode of the set of data is _____ pounds.

15. The range of the weight of the dogs is _____ pounds.

16. _____ of the dogs weigh less than 18 pounds.

17. An eighth dog is weighed at the pet-care center.
Its weight is 32 pounds. How would this change
the stem-and-leaf plot?
How would this change the median and mode?

Practice 4   Outcomes

Decide which are possible outcomes. Write *yes* or *no*.

A coin is tossed once.

1. The coin lands on heads. _____

2. The coin lands on tails. _____

3. The coin lands on both heads and tails. _____

Complete.

4. There are _____ possible outcomes when you toss a coin.

Complete. Write *more likely, less likely, certain, impossible,* or *equally likely*.

> *Example*
>
> Look at the spinner. Suppose it is spun once.
>
>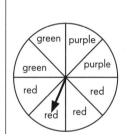
>
> It is __more likely__ that the spinner will land on red or on green.
>
> It is __equally likely__ that the spinner will land on green or on purple.
>
> It is __impossible__ that the spinner will land on yellow.
>
> It is __less likely__ that the spinner will land on green.
>
> It is __certain__ that the spinner will land on red, green, or purple.

A spinner is divided into four equal parts. The parts are red, blue, yellow, and green. The spinner is spun once.

5. It is _____ that the spinner will land on red.

6. It is _____ that the spinner will land on red, blue, yellow, or green.

7. It is _____ that the spinner will land on blue or on green.

8. It is _____ that the spinner will land on purple.

Complete each sentence.

A number cube numbered 1 to 6 is tossed once.

9. There are _____ possible outcomes.

10. The number cube lands with an even number on top. There are _____ possible outcomes.

11. The number cube lands with a number less than 3 on top. There are _____ possible outcomes.

Study the data in the table.

Three bags each contain eight colored marbles.

Number of Marbles in Three Bags

Color of Marbles	Bag A	Bag B	Bag C
Green	4	6	8
Red	4	2	0

Complete. Write *more likely, less likely, certain, impossible,* or *equally likely* to describe each outcome.

12. A green marble is drawn from Bag B. _____

13. A red marble is drawn from Bag B. _____

14. A green marble is drawn from Bag C. _____

15. A red marble is drawn from Bag C. _____

16. A red or green marble is drawn from Bag B. _____

Practice 5   Probability as a Fraction

Find the probability as a fraction in simplest form.

Jake spins the spinner once. He wants to land on these numbers.
What is the probability of a favorable outcome?

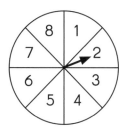

Example

He wants to land on a number less than 3.

There are 2 favorable outcomes: 1 and 2
There are 8 possible outcomes : 1, 2, 3, 4, 5, 6, 7, and 8

Probability of a favorable outcome = $\dfrac{\text{Number of favorable outcomes}}{\text{Number of possible outcomes}}$

$= \dfrac{2}{8}$

$= \dfrac{1}{4}$

1.   He wants to land on the number 7.

2.   He wants to land on an odd number.

Find the probability as a fraction in simplest form for each outcome.

A coin is tossed once. The probability of getting

3. heads is ⬚.

4. tails is ⬚.

A number cube numbered 1 to 6 is tossed once.
The probability of getting

5. the number 2 is ⬚.

6. the number 0 is ⬚.

7. an even number is ⬚.

8. a number greater than 4 is ⬚.

A circular spinner has 4 equal parts. The parts are colored
red, blue, green, and yellow. The spinner is spun once.
The probability of landing on

9. red is ⬚.

10. blue is ⬚.

11. purple is ⬚.

12. green, red, or yellow is ⬚.

13. red, blue, green, or yellow is ⬚.

Find the probability as a fraction in simplest form for each outcome.

A bag contains 10 discs numbered 1 to 10. A disc is drawn
from the bag. The probability of drawing

14. the number 10 is [ ] .

15. a number less than 5 is [ ] .

16. an odd number is [ ] .

17. a number divisible by 3 is [ ] .

18. a number greater than 8 is [ ] .

19. the number 12 is [ ] .

A bag contains 3 white marbles, 3 blue marbles, and 6 red marbles.
A marble is drawn from the bag. The probability of getting

20. a white marble is [ ] .

21. a blue marble is [ ] .

22. Which is more likely: drawing a red marble or drawing a blue marble? Explain.

Find the probability of each outcome on the number line. Then describe the outcome as *more likely, less likely, certain, impossible,* or *equally likely.*

--- Example ---

A box contains 4 red pencils, 1 blue pencil, and 1 black pencil.
Find the probability of picking a red pencil.

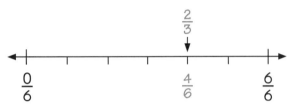

The closer the probability of an outcome is to 1, the more likely the outcome is to occur.

The probability of picking a red pencil is $\frac{4}{6}$ or $\frac{2}{3}$.

$\frac{2}{3}$ is closer to 1 than to 0 on the number line. So, the likelihood of picking a red pencil is more likely.

Each card in a set of 8 cards has a picture of a fruit. There are 3 orange cards, 2 apple cards, 2 pear cards, and 1 peach card. The cards are shuffled, placed in a stack, and one card is picked.

23. An orange card: _____

24. An apple card: _____

25. An apple, peach, or pear card: _____

26. An apple, orange, peach, or pear card: _____

Practice 6   Real-World Problems: Data and Probability

Solve. Show your work.

--- Example ---

In a test, Carl, Sarah, and Dinesh scored an average of 70 points.
Carl scored 65 and Sarah scored 82. How many points did Dinesh get?

Total score of the 3 students = 3 × 70
                              = 210 points

Carl and Sarah's total score = 65 + 82
                             = 147 points

Dinesh's test score = 210 − 147
                    = 63 points

Dinesh's test score was 63 points.

---

1.   Luis went on a fishing trip from Thursday to Sunday.
On average, he caught 12 fish per day. He caught 15 fish on Thursday.
How many fish did he catch altogether from Friday to Sunday?

2. Nicole bought 20 pieces of fabric of different lengths. The average length of 12 pieces is 3 feet. The total length of the other 8 pieces is 44 feet. Find the average length of the 20 pieces of fabric.

3. Ron drove his car every day from Monday to Saturday. On Monday and Tuesday, the car used an average of 2 gallons of gas each day. From Wednesday to Saturday, the car used an average of 3 gallons of gas each day. Find the total amount of gas the car used from Monday to Saturday.

Solve. Show your work. Use bar models to help you.

┌─ *Example* ───┐

The average number of students in Class A and Class B is 24.
Class A has 4 more students than Class B.
How many students are there in each class?

Total number of students in both classes = 2 x 24 = 48

48 − 4 = 44

44 ÷ 2 = 22 students   Class A

22 + 4 = 26 students   Class B

48

4

Class A has 26 students, and Class B has 22 students.

└──┘

4. Mrs. Johnson buys 2 chickens. The average weight of
the 2 chickens is 4 pounds. One of the chickens is
2 pounds heavier than the other. What is the weight
of the heavier chicken?

Solve. Show your work.

Example

A group of athletes took part in a charity marathon. The table shows the number of kilometers completed by each athlete.

Results of Charity Marathon

Number of Kilometers Completed by each Athlete	Number of Athletes
42	4
36	1
28	3

Find the median.

28, 28, 28, 36, 42, 42, 42, 42

The median is $\dfrac{36 + 42}{2}$ = 39 kilometers.

Find the mode.

28, 28, 28, 36, 42, 42, 42, 42

The mode is 42 kilometers.

Find the range.

The range is 42 − 28 = 14 kilometers.

Find the mean.

4 x 42 km = 168 km
1 x 36 km = 36 km
3 x 28 km = 84 km
Total = 168 + 36 + 84
       = 288 km

The mean is 288 ÷ 8 = 36 kilometers.

Another athlete joins the charity marathon and completes 27 kilometers.
Will this athlete's distance increase or decrease the mean?
Explain why you think so. Then find the new mean number of kilometers
completed by all the athletes.

*The new athlete's distance will decrease the mean because this
new data point is less than the old mean.*
288 + 27 = 315 km
315 ÷ 9 = 35 km

The new mean is 35 kilometers.

For every kilometer each athlete completed, $25 would be donated
to charity. Find the amount of money raised for charity by the 9 athletes.

315 x $25 = $7,875

The amount raised for charity is $7,875.

5. The scores of 9 players playing 18 holes of golf are 65, 72, 70, 69, 72, 67,
70, 72, and 73.

   a. Find the median score.

   b. Find the mode of the scores.

   c. Find the range of the set of data.

   d. Find the mean of the set of data.

   e. Another player scores 80. Predict how this player's score will
change the median, mode, range, and mean of the data and
explain your reasoning. Then compute each of these measures
to check your predictions.

The line plot shows Marilyn's science test scores during one semester. Each X represents one test.

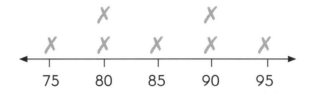

Marilyn's Science Test Scores

a. How many tests did she take?

7

b. Find the median, mode, and range of her scores.

Marilyn's median score is 85.
Marilyn's modal scores are 80 and 90.
The range of her scores is 95 − 75 = 20.

c. Find her mean score.

1 x 75 = 75
2 x 80 = 160
1 x 85 = 85
2 x 90 = 180
1 x 95 = 95
Total = 595

595 ÷ 7 = 85

Her mean score is 85.

d. After Marilyn took another test, her new mean score was 84. What was her latest score?

84 x 8 = 672
672 − 595 = 77

Her latest score was 77.

6. Kurt recorded the daily temperature highs for a science project. The results are shown in the line plot.

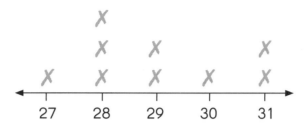

Daily Temperature Highs in °F

a. On how many days did he record the temperature?

b. What were the mean and median temperatures?

c. The temperature high on another day was included with the data. The new mean temperature changed to 30°F. What was this temperature?

d. Find the new median temperature.

7. A restaurant pays its 9 employees these daily wages:
$90, $70, $100, $90, $90, $90, $100, $160, $200
Make a line plot to show the data.

a. Find the mean and median of the set of wages.

b. Does the mean or the median better describe what a new employee could expect to earn at this restaurant?

c. Are there any outliers? If so, what are they?

d. How do the mean and median each change if you disregard the outliers? Now does the mean or median better represent what a new employee could expect to earn?

Example

During a trip to the beach, 9 children collected seashells. The stem-and-leaf plot shows the number of shells each child collected.

Number of Seashells Collected	
Stem	Leaves
6	1 1 5
7	0 6 8
8	3 8
9	?

6 | 1 = 61

a. If the total number of seashells collected is 681, find the missing number. What is the outlier?

$681 - 61 - 61 - 65 - 70 - 76 - 78 - 83 - 88 = 99$

The missing number is 99. The outlier is 99 because it is farthest from the other numbers.

b. Find the median of the set of data.

The median is 76.

c. Find the mode of the set of data.

The mode is 61.

d. Find the range of the set of data.

$99 - 61 = 38$

The range is 38.

8. The stem-and-leaf plot shows the weights of some bowling balls in pounds.

Weights of Bowling Balls (lb)	
Stem	**Leaves**
0	8 8 9
1	0 0 1 1 2 2 4 4 5 5 5 6 6 6

$$0 \mid 8 = 8$$

a. How many bowling balls are there?

b. Find the median, mode, and range.

c. What is the least number of bowling balls needed to make the mode 14 pounds?

d. Find the total weight of the bowling balls in **Exercise 8.c**.

Find the probability of each outcome on a number line. Then describe the likelihood of each outcome as *more likely*, *less likely*, *certain*, *impossible*, or *equally likely*.

9. The weather forecast in a city is that for every week, 3 days are sunny, 2 are cloudy, and 2 are rainy. On any chosen day, describe the probability of each of these outcomes.

Example

It is a sunny day.

$$\text{Probability} = \frac{\text{Number of favorable outcomes}}{\text{Number of possible outcomes}}$$

$$= \frac{3}{7}$$

Less likely

a. It is not a sunny day.

b. It is a rainy, sunny, or a cloudy day.

c. If today is sunny, tomorrow is rainy.

Solve.

10. In a class of 25 students, 10 are girls. The names of the students
are written on cards and placed in a box. The names are chosen
at random to win prizes donated by a local store.

    a. What is the probability that the first student selected is a girl?

    b. What is the probability that the first student selected is a boy?

    c. If the first student selected is a girl, what is the probability that the second
student selected is also a girl?

Math Journal

Write the steps to solve the problem.

Neil bought 5 books. The average price of 2 of the books is $5. The average price of the rest of the books is $4. Find the total amount of money Neil paid for the 5 books.

Then, following your steps above, solve the problem.

Put On Your Thinking Cap!

Challenging Practice

1. Michelle got an average score of 80 on two tests. What score must she get on the third test so that her average score for the three tests is the same as the average score for the first two tests?

2. The line plot shows the shoe sizes of students in Ms. George's class.

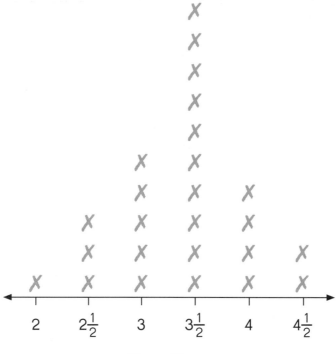

Shoe Sizes

a. How many students are in the class?

b. What is the mode of the set of data?

c. How many students in the class wear a size $3\frac{1}{2}$ shoe?

d. Suppose you looked at 100 pairs of shoes for the grade, which includes 3 other classes. How many pairs of size $3\frac{1}{2}$ would there be? Explain your answer.

Put On Your Thinking Cap!

Problem Solving

1. The average height of Andy, Chen, and Chelsea is 145 centimeters. Andy and Chen are of the same height and Chelsea is 15 centimeters taller than Andy. Find Andy's height and Chelsea's height.

2. Eduardo has 3 times as many stamps as Sally. The average number of stamps they have is 450. How many more stamps does Eduardo have than Sally?

3. Bag A and Bag B each contain 2 marbles — 1 white and 1 red. Troy picks 1 marble from Bag A and 1 from Bag B. What is the probability that the following are picked?

a. 2 white marbles

b. 1 red and 1 white marble

Chapter 6 Fractions and Mixed Numbers

Practice 1 Adding Fractions

**Find the equivalent fraction. Complete the model.
Then add.**

Example

$$\frac{3}{8} + \frac{1}{2} = \boxed{\frac{3}{8}} + \boxed{\frac{4}{8}}$$

$$= \boxed{\frac{7}{8}}$$

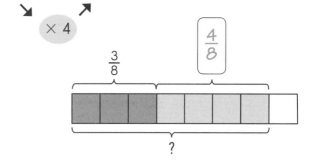

1.

$$\frac{2}{3} + \frac{2}{9} = \frac{\boxed{}}{\boxed{}} + \frac{\boxed{}}{\boxed{}}$$

$$= \boxed{}$$

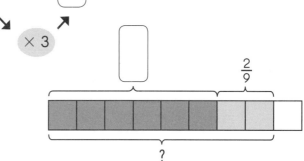

Add. Write each answer in simplest form.

2. $\dfrac{3}{5} + \dfrac{3}{10} = \dfrac{\boxed{}}{\boxed{}} + \dfrac{\boxed{}}{\boxed{}}$

$= \boxed{}$

3. $\dfrac{5}{12} + \dfrac{1}{3} = \dfrac{\boxed{}}{\boxed{}} + \dfrac{\boxed{}}{\boxed{}}$

$= \boxed{}$

$= \boxed{}$

4. Find the sum of $\dfrac{1}{6}$ and $\dfrac{1}{12}$.

5. Add $\dfrac{1}{4}$ to the answer in **Exercise 4**.

6. What is the sum of $\dfrac{1}{8}$, $\dfrac{1}{4}$, and $\dfrac{3}{8}$?

7. Add $\dfrac{1}{3}$, $\dfrac{3}{12}$, and $\dfrac{5}{12}$.

Practice 2   Subtracting Fractions

**Find the equivalent fraction. Complete the model.
Then subtract.**

Example

$$\frac{5}{8} - \frac{1}{2} = \frac{\boxed{5}}{\boxed{8}} - \frac{\boxed{4}}{\boxed{8}}$$

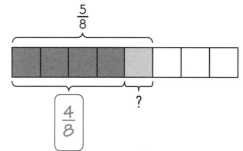

$$\frac{1}{2} = \frac{\boxed{4}}{\boxed{8}}$$

$$= \boxed{\frac{1}{8}}$$

$$\overset{\frac{5}{8}}{\overbrace{\qquad\qquad\qquad}}$$

$$\underset{\boxed{\frac{4}{8}}}{\underbrace{\qquad\qquad}}\; ?$$

1.

$$\frac{2}{3} - \frac{2}{9} = \frac{\boxed{}}{\boxed{}} - \frac{\boxed{}}{\boxed{}}$$

$$\frac{2}{3} = \frac{\boxed{}}{\boxed{}}$$ (× 3)

$$= \boxed{}$$

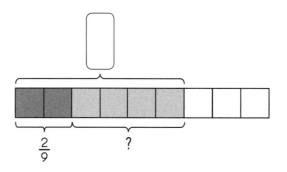

$$\underset{\frac{2}{9}}{\underbrace{\qquad}}\;\underset{?}{\underbrace{\qquad\qquad}}$$

Subtract. Write each answer in simplest form.

2. $\dfrac{8}{10} - \dfrac{1}{5} = \dfrac{\boxed{}}{\boxed{}} - \dfrac{\boxed{}}{\boxed{}}$

$= \boxed{}$

$= \boxed{}$

3. $\dfrac{7}{12} - \dfrac{1}{4} = \dfrac{\boxed{}}{\boxed{}} - \dfrac{\boxed{}}{\boxed{}}$

$= \boxed{}$

$= \boxed{}$

4. The difference between $\dfrac{7}{8}$ and $\dfrac{1}{4}$ is $\boxed{}$.

5. The difference between $\dfrac{7}{12}$ and $\dfrac{1}{3}$ is $\boxed{}$.

Practice 3   Mixed Numbers

Write a mixed number for each model.

Example

  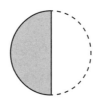

1 whole   1 whole   1 half

When you add a whole number and a fraction, you get a mixed number.

$2 + \dfrac{1}{2} = \boxed{2\dfrac{1}{2}}$

1.

 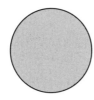 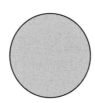 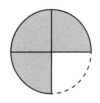

1 whole   1 whole   1 whole   3 fourths

$3 + \dfrac{3}{4} = \boxed{}$

2.

1 whole   1 whole   1 whole   2 fifths

$3 + \dfrac{2}{5} = \boxed{}$

Write a mixed number for each model.

3.

☐ wholes and ☐ half is ☐ .

4.

☐ whole and ☐ fifths is ☐ .

5.

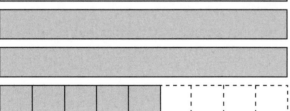

☐ wholes and ☐ ninths is ☐ .

Check (✔) the correct model.

6. Which model shows $1\frac{3}{4}$ shaded?

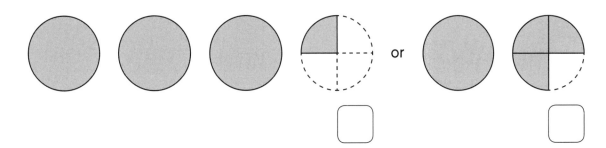

or

7. Which model shows $2\frac{3}{5}$ shaded?

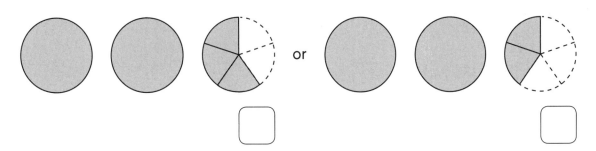

or

Write each answer as a mixed number.

8. $4 + \dfrac{1}{4} = \boxed{}$

9. $3 + \dfrac{5}{9} = \boxed{}$

10. $\dfrac{5}{8} + 2 = \boxed{}$

11. $\dfrac{3}{5} + 4 = \boxed{}$

Write the correct mixed number in each box.

12.

0 $\frac{1}{7}$ $\frac{2}{7}$ $\frac{3}{7}$ $\frac{4}{7}$ $\frac{5}{7}$ $\frac{6}{7}$ 1 $1\frac{1}{7}$ $1\frac{2}{7}$ ↑ $1\frac{6}{7}$ 2 $2\frac{1}{7}$ $2\frac{4}{7}$ ↑ 3

Write a mixed number for each item.

13. The pears have a weight of

[   ] pounds.

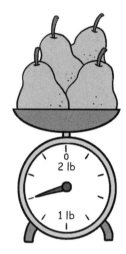

14. The worm started crawling from 0 centimeters.

It has crawled [   ] centimeters.

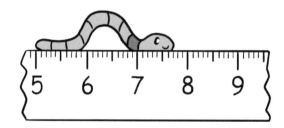

Write each mixed number in simplest form.

Example

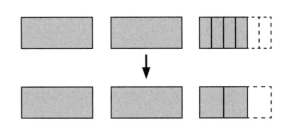

$1\frac{2}{4} = \boxed{1\frac{1}{2}}$

15.

$2\frac{4}{6} = \boxed{}$

16. $3\frac{4}{8} = \boxed{}$

17. $5\frac{6}{9} = \boxed{}$

18. $6\frac{4}{12} = \boxed{}$

19. $4\frac{3}{6} = \boxed{}$

Write each fraction and mixed number in a box to show its correct location on the number line.

20. $1\frac{1}{2}$ **21.** $\frac{1}{2}$ **22.** $1\frac{3}{4}$

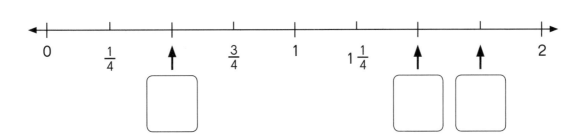

Fill in the boxes with fractions or mixed numbers.
Express each answer in simplest form.

Example

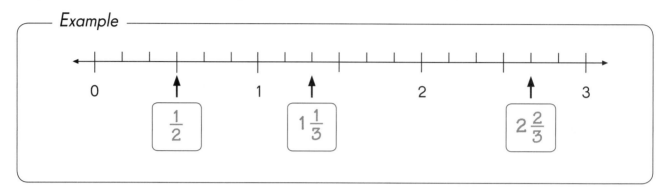

23.

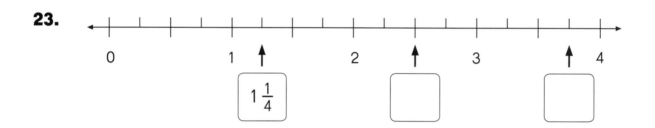

24.

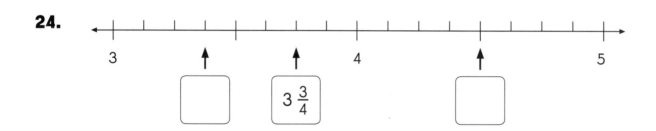

25.

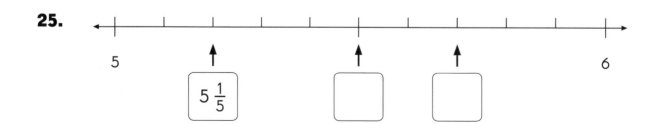

Practice 4   Improper Fractions

Write each mixed number as an improper fraction.

┌─ *Example* ───┐

$1\frac{2}{3}$

$1 = $ _____3_____ thirds

$\frac{2}{3} = $ _____2_____ thirds

$1\frac{2}{3} = $ _____5_____ thirds

$= \boxed{\dfrac{5}{3}}$

An improper fraction is equal to or greater than 1.

└──┘

1.

$2\frac{3}{4}$

$2 = $ _____ fourths

$\frac{3}{4} = $ _____ fourths

$2\frac{3}{4} = $ _____ fourths

$= \boxed{}$

2.

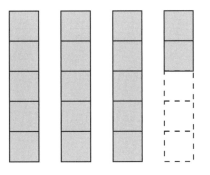

$3\frac{2}{5}$

$3 = $ _____ fifths

$\frac{2}{5} = $ _____ fifths

$3\frac{2}{5} = $ _____ fifths

$= \boxed{}$

Write the improper fractions for the shaded parts.

3.

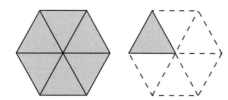

There are _____ sixths in $1\frac{1}{6}$.

$1\frac{1}{6} = \boxed{} + \boxed{} + \boxed{} + \boxed{} + \boxed{} + \boxed{} + \boxed{}$

$= \boxed{}$

4.

$2\frac{3}{8} = \boxed{}$

5.

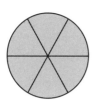

$2\frac{5}{6} = \boxed{}$

Name: _____ **Date:** _____

Write the improper fraction for the shaded parts.

6.

$3\frac{3}{5} =$ ☐

Write a mixed number and an improper fraction for each model.

┌─ *Example* ──┐

Mixed number: $1\frac{3}{4}$ Improper fraction: $\frac{7}{4}$

└──┘

7.

Mixed number: ☐   Improper fraction: ☐

8.

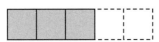

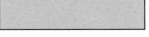

Mixed number: ☐   Improper fraction: ☐

Write a mixed number and an improper fraction for each model.

9.

Mixed number: ☐   Improper fraction: ☐

Write the missing improper fraction in each box.
Express the answers in simplest form.

10.

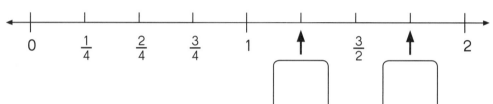

11.

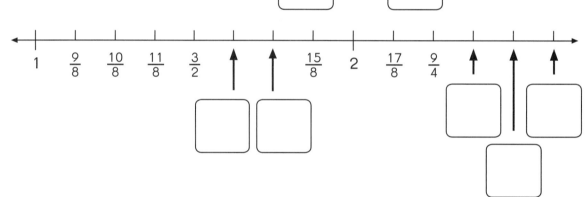

Write each improper fraction in a box to show its correct location
on the number line.

12. $\frac{4}{3}$ **13.** $\frac{7}{3}$ **14.** $\frac{17}{9}$

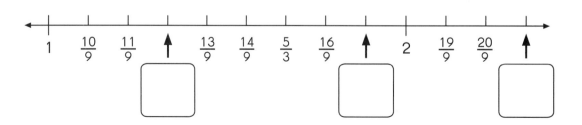

Practice 5   Renaming Improper Fractions and Mixed Numbers

Express each improper fraction as a mixed number.

Example

$$\frac{8}{5} = \frac{5}{5} + \frac{\boxed{3}}{5}$$

$$= 1 + \frac{\boxed{3}}{5}$$

$$= 1\frac{\boxed{3}}{5}$$

1. $\frac{12}{7} = \frac{\boxed{}}{7} + \frac{\boxed{}}{7}$

$$= 1 + \frac{\boxed{}}{7}$$

$$= 1\frac{\boxed{}}{7}$$

2. $\frac{9}{4} = \frac{\boxed{}}{4} + \frac{\boxed{}}{4}$

$$= 2 + \frac{\boxed{}}{4}$$

$$= 2\frac{\boxed{}}{4}$$

3. $\frac{13}{6} = \frac{\boxed{}}{6} + \frac{\boxed{}}{6}$

$$= 2 + \frac{\boxed{}}{6}$$

$$= 2\frac{\boxed{}}{6}$$

Express each improper fraction as a mixed number.

Example

$$\frac{9}{2} = \boxed{4\frac{1}{2}}$$

$$\begin{array}{r} 4 \\ 2\overline{)9} \\ \underline{8} \\ 1 \end{array}$$

Use the division rule.
$9 \div 2 = 4\,R\,1$

4. $\frac{17}{4} = \boxed{}$

5. $\frac{29}{6} = \boxed{}$

Express each improper fraction as a whole number or a mixed number in simplest form. Show your work.

6. $\dfrac{9}{6}$ = ☐ + ☐

   = ☐ + ☐

   = ☐

   = ☐

7. $\dfrac{12}{4}$ = ☐

8. $\dfrac{21}{3}$ = ☐

9. $\dfrac{14}{4}$ = ☐

   = ☐

10. $\dfrac{15}{6}$ = ☐

    = ☐

Express each mixed number as an improper fraction.

Example

$$2\frac{3}{5} = \boxed{2} + \frac{3}{5}$$

$$= \frac{\boxed{10}}{5} + \frac{3}{5}$$

$$= \frac{\boxed{13}}{5}$$

11. $3\frac{5}{9} = 3 + \frac{\boxed{}}{9}$

$$= \frac{\boxed{}}{9} + \frac{\boxed{}}{9}$$

$$= \frac{\boxed{}}{9}$$

12. $2\frac{5}{8} = \boxed{} + \frac{5}{8}$

$$= \frac{\boxed{}}{8} + \frac{5}{8}$$

$$= \frac{\boxed{}}{8}$$

13. $4\frac{2}{7} = 4 + \frac{\boxed{}}{7}$

$$= \frac{\boxed{}}{7} + \frac{\boxed{}}{7}$$

$$= \frac{\boxed{}}{7}$$

Express each mixed number as an improper fraction.

Example

$$2\frac{1}{5} = \boxed{\frac{11}{5}}$$

Use the multiplication rule:
2 × 5 = 10
10 + 1 = 11
There are 11 fifths in $2\frac{1}{5}$.

14. $2\frac{3}{8} = \boxed{}$

15. $3\frac{3}{4} = \boxed{}$

16. $6\frac{2}{5} = \boxed{}$

17. $2\frac{4}{7} = \boxed{}$

Express each mixed number as an improper fraction and each improper fraction as a mixed or whole number. Then solve the riddle.

18. $\dfrac{9}{7}$ = [   ] (b)

19. $\dfrac{15}{6}$ = [   ] (o)

20. $\dfrac{14}{7}$ = [ ] (a)

21. $2\dfrac{2}{7}$ = [   ] (i)

22. $3\dfrac{5}{8}$ = [   ] (t)

23. $5\dfrac{3}{5}$ = [   ] (r)

Which two animals can look behind without turning their heads?
Write the letters which match the answers to find out.

P _____ _____ _____ _____ _____
      2     $\dfrac{28}{5}$ $\dfrac{28}{5}$ $2\dfrac{1}{2}$ $\dfrac{29}{8}$

and

   _____ _____ _____ _____ _____ _____
    $\dfrac{28}{5}$ 2 $1\dfrac{2}{7}$ $1\dfrac{2}{7}$ $\dfrac{16}{7}$ $\dfrac{29}{8}$

Practice 6   Renaming Whole Numbers when Adding and Subtracting Fractions

Fill in the missing numerators.

Example

$$3 = 2\frac{\boxed{4}}{4} = 1\frac{\boxed{8}}{4} = \frac{\boxed{12}}{4}$$

1. $3 = 2\dfrac{\boxed{}}{6}$

$= 1\dfrac{\boxed{}}{6}$

$= \dfrac{\boxed{}}{6}$

2. $2\dfrac{7}{9} = 1\dfrac{\boxed{}}{9}$

$= \dfrac{\boxed{}}{9}$

Add. Express each answer as a mixed number in simplest form.

3. $\dfrac{4}{9} + \dfrac{2}{3}$

4. $\dfrac{1}{6} + \dfrac{11}{12}$

5. $\dfrac{1}{4} + \dfrac{3}{8} + \dfrac{3}{4}$

6. $\dfrac{4}{5} + \dfrac{7}{10} + \dfrac{9}{10}$

Subtract. Express each answer as a mixed number in simplest form.

Example

$2 - \dfrac{1}{3}$

Method 1

$$2 - \dfrac{1}{3} = \dfrac{2}{1} - \dfrac{1}{3}$$
$$= \dfrac{6}{3} - \dfrac{1}{3}$$
$$= \dfrac{5}{3} = 1\dfrac{2}{3}$$

Method 2

$$2 - \dfrac{1}{3} = 1\dfrac{3}{3} - \dfrac{1}{3}$$
$$= 1\dfrac{2}{3}$$

7. $\quad 3 - \dfrac{5}{6} - \dfrac{1}{3}$

8. $\quad 2 - \dfrac{1}{4} - \dfrac{1}{4}$

9. $\quad 2 - \dfrac{2}{7} - \dfrac{3}{14}$

10. $\quad 3 - \dfrac{7}{10} - \dfrac{3}{5}$

Practice 7   Fraction of a Set

Check (✔) the box next to the group of shapes that show $\frac{3}{5}$ shaded.

1.

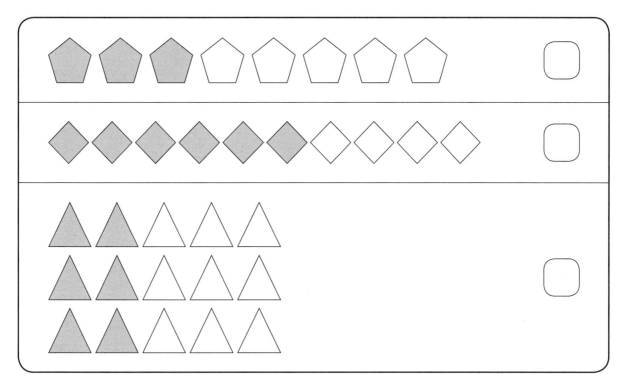

What fraction of each set of shapes is shaded? Express your answer in simplest form.

Example

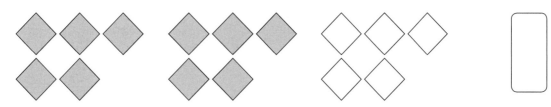

$\frac{3}{4}$

2.

3.

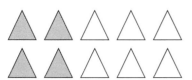

Use a model to help you answer each question.

Example

What is $\frac{2}{3}$ of 18?

3 units ⟶ __18__

1 unit ⟶ __6__

2 units ⟶ __12__

So, $\frac{2}{3}$ of 18 = __12__.

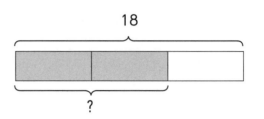

---

4. What is $\frac{3}{4}$ of 16?

4 units ⟶ _____

1 unit ⟶ _____

3 units ⟶ _____

So, $\frac{3}{4}$ of 16 = _____.

Model:

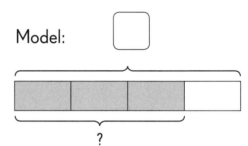

---

5. What is $\frac{2}{5}$ of 25?

_____ units ⟶ _____

1 unit ⟶ _____

_____ units ⟶ _____

So, $\frac{2}{5}$ of 25 = _____.

Model:

Use a model to help you answer the question.

6. What is $\frac{5}{6}$ of 30?

_____ units $\longrightarrow$ _____   Model :

1 unit $\longrightarrow$ _____

_____ units $\longrightarrow$ _____

So, $\frac{5}{6}$ of 30 = _____.

Solve.

> *Example*
>
> $\frac{2}{3} \times 15$
>
> $\frac{2}{3}$ of 15 is ___10___.

7. $\frac{3}{4} \times 12$

$\frac{3}{4}$ of 12 is _____.

8. $\frac{2}{5} \times 20$

$\frac{2}{5}$ of 20 is _____.

9. $\frac{6}{7} \times 42$

$\frac{6}{7}$ of 42 is _____.

Fill in the blanks to solve each problem.

Example

$$\frac{1}{2} \text{ of } 18 = \frac{1}{2} \times 18$$

$$= \underline{\frac{1 \times 18}{2}}$$

$$= \underline{\frac{18}{2}}$$

$$= \underline{\hspace{0.3cm} 9 \hspace{0.3cm}}$$

10. $\frac{2}{3}$ of $24 = \frac{2}{3} \times$ _____

$$= \underline{\hspace{2cm}}$$

$$= \underline{\hspace{2cm}}$$

$$= \underline{\hspace{2cm}}$$

11. $\frac{3}{4}$ of $32 =$ _____ $\times 32$

$$= \underline{\hspace{2cm}}$$

$$= \underline{\hspace{2cm}}$$

$$= \underline{\hspace{2cm}}$$

Write each answer in the box. Then solve the riddle.

12. $\frac{1}{4} \times 28 = \boxed{}$ ·········· (l)

13. $\frac{2}{3} \times 21 = \boxed{}$ ·········· (o)

14. $\frac{2}{5} \times 50 = \boxed{}$ ·········· (s)

15. $\frac{3}{4} \times 24 = \boxed{}$ ·········· (a)

16. $\frac{5}{6} \times 30 = \boxed{}$ ·········· (a)

17. $\frac{6}{7} \times 35 = \boxed{}$ ·········· (k)

Which animals often sleep about 18 to 20 hours a day?
Write the letters that match the answers to find out.

_____	_____	_____	_____	_____	_____
30	14	25	7	18	20

Practice 8 Real-World Problems: Fractions

Solve. Show your work.

Example

Ali bought three packets of dried fruit.

$\frac{1}{3}$ lb $\frac{1}{3}$ lb $\frac{1}{6}$ lb

What is the total weight of all three packets of dried fruit?

$\frac{1}{3} + \frac{1}{3} + \frac{1}{6}$

$$\frac{1}{3} \overset{\times 2}{\underset{\times 2}{=}} \frac{2}{6}$$

$\frac{2}{6} + \frac{2}{6} + \frac{1}{6} = \frac{5}{6}$

The total weight of all three packets of dried fruit is $\frac{5}{6}$ pound.

Solve. Show your work.

1. Jim had three waffles.

    He ate $\frac{1}{6}$ of one waffle, and $\frac{2}{3}$ of another waffle.

    How many waffles were left?

2. A grocery store has 5 pounds of granola. One customer buys

    $\frac{2}{3}$ pound of granola and another buys $\frac{5}{6}$ pound.

    After these purchases, how much granola is left?

3. Karen jogs $\frac{1}{2}$ mile. Selma jogs $\frac{1}{4}$ mile more than Karen.

Lena jogs $\frac{3}{4}$ mile more than Selma. How far does Lena jog?

4. Jeremy has 18 marbles. He loses 6 of them.

a. What fraction of the marbles does he lose?

b. What fraction of the marbles does he have left?

5. Mrs. Yan buys 4 red tulips and 5 yellow tulips.

    a. What fraction of the tulips are red?

    b. What fraction of the tulips are yellow?

6. Charles owns 3 cats, 4 goldfish, and some parakeets.
Altogether, he has 10 pets.

    a. What fraction of his pets are goldfish?

    b. What fraction of his pets are parakeets?

7. Rick had $20. He spent $10 on food, $6 on a movie ticket and saved the rest.

    a. How much money did he save?

    b. What fraction of the total amount did he save?

8. There are 24 boys in a class, and $\frac{2}{3}$ of the students in the class are boys. How many students are girls?

9. One morning, The Shirt Shop sold 15 T-shirts.

Of the T-shirts sold, $\frac{1}{5}$ were gray. The rest were white.

How many white T-shirts were sold?

10. A chef bought some green and red peppers. She bought

18 green peppers, which was $\frac{3}{4}$ of the total number.

  a. How many red peppers did she buy?

  b. How many peppers did she buy altogether?

11.   There were 25 melons in a box at the grocery store.

The store sold $\frac{3}{5}$ of the melons.

How many melons were sold?

12.   Ava read $\frac{1}{4}$ of a book on Monday, and $\frac{1}{5}$ of it on Tuesday.

There are 80 pages in the book.

How many pages did she read altogether on both days?

Math Journal

Is the model correct? If not, explain why it is wrong. Draw the correct model.

Example

$\frac{1}{4}$ of 12

12

The model is wrong because it should have only four parts.

Correct model:

12

$\frac{2}{7}$ of 21

21

_____

_____

Correct model:

Put On Your Thinking Cap!

Challenging Practice

1. Show $1\frac{1}{4}$ shaded, if 1 whole is made up of 4 squares.

Some of the shading has been done for you.

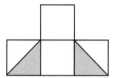 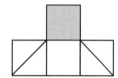

2. Is the answer of $21 \times \frac{2}{7}$ the same as that of $2 \times \frac{21}{7}$?
Show your work.

3. Write a fraction and a whole number that have the same product as the problem below.

$$8 \times \frac{3}{4} = \text{_____}$$

$$\text{_____} \times \text{_____} = \text{_____}$$

Put On Your Thinking Cap!

Problem Solving

Caroline places five poles A, B, C, D, and E in order along a straight line. The distance between poles A and D is 1 yard. The distance between poles B and C is the same as the distance between poles A and B.

Poles A and B are $\frac{1}{5}$ yard apart.

The distance between D and E is $\frac{7}{10}$ yard.

How far apart are poles B and E?

Cumulative Review

for Chapters 5 and 6

Concepts and Skills

Complete. Use the data in the table. *(Lesson 5.1)*

The ages of four cousins are shown.

8, 12, 10, 6

1. The sum of their ages is _____ years.

2. The mean age of the cousins is _____ years.

Answer each question. Use the data in the line plot. *(Lesson 5.2)*

A group of hikers made a line plot to show the number of mountains they climbed. Each X represents one hiker.

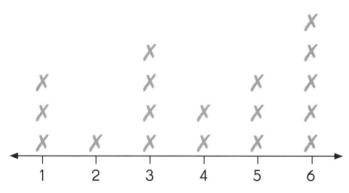

Number of Mountains Climbed

3. What is the median number of mountains climbed? _____

4. What is the range of the set of data? _____

5. What is the mode of the set of data? _____

Make a stem-and-leaf plot to show the data. (Lesson 5.3)

6. A group of friends went bowling and recorded these scores.

| 75 | 73 | 79 | 84 | 98 | 64 | 84 | 67 |

Bowling Scores	
Stem	**Leaves**

$9|8 = 98$

Complete. Use the data in your stem-and-leaf plot.

7. _____ is the mode.

8. _____ is the median.

9. _____ is the range.

10. _____ is an outlier.

11. How do the mode and median each change if you disregard the outlier?

_____

_____

Write *more likely, less likely, equally likely, certain,* or *impossible*. *(Lesson 5.4)*

A bag has 8 blue marbles and 2 orange marbles. Describe the likelihood of each outcome.

12. An orange marble is chosen. _____

13. A blue marble is chosen. _____

14. A red marble is chosen. _____

15. A blue or an orange marble is chosen. _____

Solve. Use the scenario above. *(Lesson 5.4)*

16. How would you change the number of each colored marble in the bag so that it is more likely that an orange marble is chosen?

Look at the spinner. Write the probability of each outcome as a fraction. *(Lesson 5.5)*

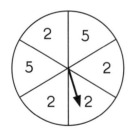

17. Probability of landing on 2 = ☐

18. Probability of landing on 6 = ☐

Add or subtract. Write each answer in simplest form. *(Lessons 6.1 and 6.2)*

19. $\frac{3}{4} + \frac{1}{12} + \frac{1}{6} =$

20. $\frac{9}{10} - \frac{1}{5} - \frac{1}{2} =$

Write the amount of water in each set of 1-liter containers as a mixed number. *(Lesson 6.3)*

21.

  L

22.

   L

Express the shaded part of each figure as a mixed number or an improper fraction. *(Lessons 6.4 and 6.5)*

23.

$2\frac{3}{4}$ or

24.

or $\frac{12}{8}$

Express each improper fraction as a mixed number. *(Lesson 6.5)*

25. $\dfrac{9}{7} =$ ☐

26. $\dfrac{20}{9} =$ ☐

Express each mixed number as an improper fraction. *(Lesson 6.5)*

27. $3\dfrac{2}{5} =$ ☐

28. $2\dfrac{8}{9} =$ ☐

Add or subtract. *(Lesson 6.6)*

29. $2 + \dfrac{2}{5} + \dfrac{1}{10} =$ ☐

30. $3 - \dfrac{3}{4} - \dfrac{5}{8} =$ ☐

Check (✔) each set in which $\dfrac{2}{5}$ of the figures are shaded. *(Lesson 6.7)*

31.

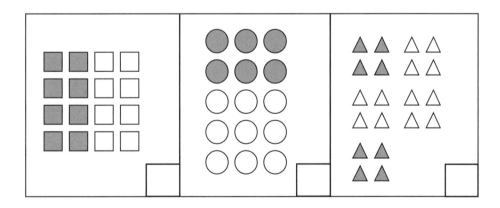

Solve. *(Lesson 6.7)*

32. $\dfrac{2}{3}$ of $15 =$ _____

33. $\dfrac{3}{5}$ of $40 =$ _____

Problem Solving

Solve. Show your work.

34. Teams A, B, C, and D were in a tournament. The average score of the 4 teams was 92. Team A scored 78 points, Team B scored 95 points, and Team C scored 88 points.

   a. How many points did Team D score?

   b. Find the range of the scores. Hence, state the difference in score between the winning team and the losing team.

35. Michael scored 15, 21, and 24 in the first three basketball games of the season.

   a. What is his mean score?

   b. What is the range of his scores?

   c. How many points must he score in the next game to achieve a mean score of 27?

36. Samuel and Kenneth collect sports cards. The average number of cards they have is 248. Samuel has 3 times as many cards as Kenneth. How many cards does each boy have?

37. A group of students made a list of the states where they were born. The line plot shows the number of times the letter 'A' appears in the name of each state. Each ✗ represents one state.

Number of Times Letter A Appears

Complete. Use the data in the line plot.

a. What is the mode of the set of data? _____

b. What is the mean number of times the letter 'A' appears? _____

c. Is the name of a state more likely to have 1 or 2 'A's? Explain your answer.

_____

_____

d. According to the data, what is less likely to happen? Explain your answer.

_____

_____

38. The stem-and-leaf plot shows the number of pages in 8 books.

Number of Pages	
Stem	**Leaves**
2	1 5
3	0 5 5 7
4	3 6

$$2|1 = 21$$

a. Which stem has only odd numbers for its leaves? _____

b. Find the median of the set of data. _____

c. Find the mode of the set of data. _____

d. Find the range of the set of data. _____

e. Which of the above measures tells you the difference in the number of

pages between the thickest and the thinnest books? _____

f. Is there an outlier in the set of data?
Explain your answer.

_____

_____

39.   A cube is numbered from 1 to 6 and tossed once. What is the probability of tossing

a.   a 5 or a 6?

b.   an odd number?

40.   Sasha has 40 stamps in her collection. 12 of them are from foreign countries.

a.   What fraction of the stamps are foreign stamps?

b.   What fraction of the stamps are U.S. stamps?

41. A string is 1 foot long. Blake cuts off 3 inches of the string. What fraction of the string is left?

42. Pedro scored $\frac{1}{4}$ of all the goals scored during a soccer game. He scored 2 goals. How many goals were not scored by Pedro?

Mid-Year Review

Test Prep

Multiple Choice

Fill in the circle next to the correct answer.

1. 13 thousands + 4 tens + 8 ones in standard form is _____. *(Lesson 1.1)*
   - Ⓐ 1,348
   - Ⓑ 10,348
   - Ⓒ 13,048
   - Ⓓ 13,480

2. In the number 83,415 the value of the digit 3 is _____. *(Lesson 1.1)*
   - Ⓐ 30
   - Ⓑ 300
   - Ⓒ 3,000
   - Ⓓ 30,000

3. 1,000 more than 37,568 is _____. *(Lesson 1.2)*
   - Ⓐ 36,568
   - Ⓑ 37,468
   - Ⓒ 37,668
   - Ⓓ 38,568

4. Estimate 681 − 307 by rounding to the nearest 100. *(Lesson 2.1)*
   - Ⓐ 300
   - Ⓑ 370
   - Ⓒ 374
   - Ⓓ 400

5. Which is the greatest common factor of 27 and 45? *(Lesson 2.2)*
   - Ⓐ 1
   - Ⓑ 3
   - Ⓒ 9
   - Ⓓ 45

6. Which pair of numbers has both a prime and a composite number? *(Lesson 2.2)*
   - Ⓐ 4 and 7
   - Ⓑ 3 and 13
   - Ⓒ 14 and 28
   - Ⓓ 6 and 8

7. What is the sum of the first two multiples of 6? *(Lesson 2.3)*

(A) 3   (B) 6

(C) 12   (D) 18

8. Mr. Finch exercises at the gym every two days. Mr. Chavez exercises at the gym every five days. When will they meet next if they first met on January 5? *(Lesson 2.3)*

(A) January 7   (B) January 10

(C) January 15   (D) January 25

9. Divide 5,613 by 7. The remainder is _____. *(Lesson 3.4)*

(A) 1   (B) 6

(C) 18   (D) 81

10. After using 35 jars to store 14 marbles each, Ali has 3 marbles left. How many marbles did he have at first? *(Lesson 3.5)*

(A) 52   (B) 178

(C) 490   (D) 493

11. The table shows the medals different teams won at a competition. *(Lesson 4.2)*

Number of Medals Won

Team	Gold	Silver	Bronze
Sandcastle	3	5	8
Coral Reef	6	1	5
Sunshine	2	4	3
Sea Horse	5	2	6

At which intersection was one medal won?

(A) Sandcastle and Gold   (B) Coral Reef and Silver

(C) Sunshine and Bronze   (D) Seahorse and Silver

12. Find the mode. *(Lesson 5.2)*

| 31 lb | 36 lb | 21 lb | 40 lb | 38 lb | 40 lb |

(A) 31 lb (B) 36 lb

(C) 37 lb (D) 40 lb

13. Jim ordered cans of fruit cocktail for his diner for 6 months. *(Lesson 5.3)*

Cans of Fruit Cocktail	
Stem	**Leaves**
2	6 9
3	1 3 3
4	0

$2|6 = 26$

What is the median number of cans he ordered?

(A) 29 cans (B) 32 cans

(C) 33 cans (D) 40 cans

14. A bag contains 5 yellow balls and 3 green balls. Choose the correct word to describe the likelihood of drawing a yellow ball from the bag. *(Lesson 5.4)*

(A) Impossible (B) Certain

(C) More likely (D) Less likely

15. Stacy draws one of these number cards from a bag.

| 12 | 8 | 5 | 16 | 10 | 3 |

What is the probability that she draws a number less than 10? *(Lesson 5.5)*

(A) $\frac{1}{2}$ (B) $\frac{1}{3}$

(C) $\frac{2}{3}$ (D) $\frac{1}{6}$

16. Which two fractions have a sum of $\frac{9}{10}$? *(Lesson 6.1)*

(A) $\frac{1}{2}$ and $\frac{4}{10}$ (B) $\frac{1}{2}$ and $\frac{1}{10}$

(C) $\frac{2}{5}$ and $\frac{1}{10}$ (D) $\frac{3}{4}$ and $\frac{6}{6}$

17. Which mixed number is represented by **A** on the number line? *(Lesson 6.3)*

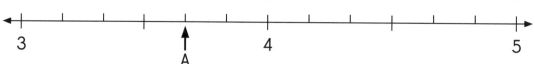

(A) $3\frac{4}{5}$ (B) $3\frac{2}{3}$

(C) $4\frac{1}{3}$ (D) $4\frac{2}{3}$

18. How many fifths are in $2\frac{3}{5}$? *(Lesson 6.4)*

(A) 10   (B) 11

(C) 13   (D) 23

19. Express $\frac{14}{6}$ as a mixed number in simplest form. *(Lesson 6.5)*

(A) $1\frac{4}{6}$ (B) $1\frac{2}{3}$

(C) $2\frac{2}{6}$ (D) $2\frac{1}{3}$

20. Ms. Lee cut a piece of yarn into different fractional parts:
$\frac{1}{12}, \frac{1}{4}$ and $\frac{5}{12}$. What fraction of the yarn is left? *(Lesson 6.7)*

(A) $\frac{1}{4}$ (B) $\frac{5}{12}$

(C) $\frac{8}{12}$ (D) $\frac{3}{4}$

Short Answer

Read each question carefully. Write your answer in the space provided. Give your answers in the correct units.

21. Write forty thousand, sixteen in expanded form. *(Lesson 1.1)*

_____

22. Arrange the numbers in order from least to greatest. *(Lesson 1.2)*

| 6,407 | | 19,999 | | 6,047 | | 20,005 |

_____

23. Estimate the quotient of 713 ÷ 9. *(Lesson 2.1)*

_____

24. The table shows the number of people who visited the space ride at a theme park. Complete the table. *(Lesson 4.2)*

Number of Visitors at the Space Ride

	Male	Female	Total
Adults	18		50
Children	32	38	

Use the table to answer Exercises 25 and 26.

25. How many people visited the space ride? *(Lesson 4.2)* _____

26. What fraction of the people who visited the space ride were children? *(Lesson 6.7)*

_____

The line graph shows the number of visitors at a museum during the course of a day. *(Lesson 4.3)*

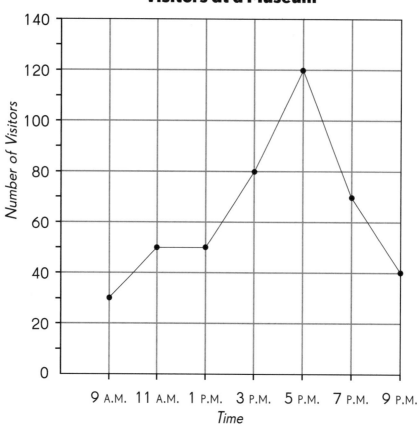

Visitors at a Museum

27. By how much did the visitor population increase from

    1:00 P.M. to 3:00 P.M.? _____

28. During which interval did the visitor population decrease the most?

    _____

29. During which interval did the same number of visitors arrive and depart?

    _____

Use the line plot to solve Exercises 30 and 31. (Lesson 5.2)

The line plot shows the number of siblings each student in John's class has.

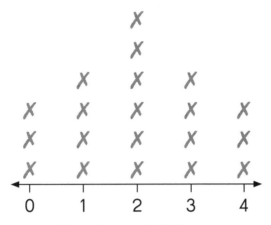

Number of Siblings

30.   Find the median of the set of data.   _____

31.   Find the mode of the set of data.   _____

Use the stem-and-leaf plot to solve Exercises 32 and 33. (Lesson 5.3)

The stem-and-leaf plot shows the number of orchids produced by 10 greenhouse plants in one month.

Number of Orchids	
Stem	**Leaves**
0	8 9
1	5 5 6
2	0 2 3 4
3	9

$0 | 8 = 8$

32.   The median of the set of data is _____.

33.   The outlier of the set of data is _____.

Look at the spinner. Write *more likely*, *less likely*, *equally likely*, *certain*, or *impossible*. Explain your answer. *(Lesson 5.4)*

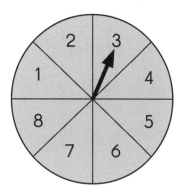

34. The spinner is _____ to land on an odd number or an even number.

Reason: _____

_____

The bar graph shows the color of the horses at a horse show.

Color of Horses at a Show

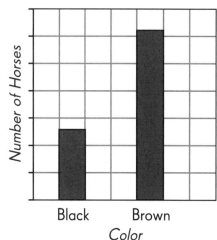

35. Which set is more likely to be the one shown in the bar graph? *(Lesson 5.4)*

Color of Horses at a Show

Color	Black	Brown
Set A	5	3
Set B	10	10
Set C	15	34

_____

Answer each question.

36. A bag has 5 red beads, 8 green beads, and 4 yellow beads. What is the probability of drawing a yellow bead from the bag? *(Lesson 5.5)*

37. Find the sum of $\frac{1}{6}$, $\frac{1}{6}$, and $\frac{2}{3}$. *(Lesson 6.1)*

38. What is $1\frac{1}{4} - \frac{5}{8}$? *(Lesson 6.6)*

39. A container and 6 lemons have a total weight of $\frac{4}{5}$ pound. Two lemons have a total weight of $\frac{1}{10}$ pound. Find the weight of the container if all the lemons have the same weight. *(Lesson 6.8)*

_____

Extended Response

Solve. Show your work.

40. A clinic needs 1,350 chairs for a charity event. Three stores donate chairs. Store A donates 216 chairs, Store B donates 420 chairs, and Store C donates 376 chairs. Does the clinic have enough chairs? Decide if you need to find an estimate or an exact answer. *(Lesson 2.1)*

41. Barrie had some stamps. He gave $\frac{1}{8}$ of them to Tom. If he gave 15 stamps to Tom, how many stamps did he have at first? *(Lesson 6.8)*

42.   Mr. Marchez ordered 7 books through a website. The total mass of the books was 3,458 grams. The masses of each book were

360 g   410 g   280 g   150 g   550 g   ?   ?

The masses of the remaining 2 books were not given. *(Lesson 5.6)*

a.   Find the mean mass of the books.

b.   Find the mean mass of the 2 remaining books.

c.   The range of the masses is 710 grams, and the lightest mass is given above. What is the mass of the heaviest book?

43. A factory packages 4,250 boxes of cereal. The number of oat cereal boxes is 715 more than the number of wheat cereal boxes. The number of fruit cereal boxes is 5 times the number of wheat cereal boxes. How many fruit cereal boxes does the factory package? *(Lesson 3.5)*

44. Three people guess the number of cherries in a bag, rounded to the nearest 10. Alex guesses 80 cherries, Jess guesses 60 cherries, and Nia guesses 70 cherries. The actual number is a multiple of 7. The sum of the digits of the number is 9.
Who guessed correctly? *(Lesson 2.1 and 2.2)*

BLANK